A Rescued
Journey

A Rescued Journey

LINDA GREENE-DUPRE

XULON PRESS

Xulon Press
2301 Lucien Way #415
Maitland, FL 32751
407.339.4217
www.xulonpress.com

Unless otherwise indicated, Scripture quotations taken from the New King James Version (NKJV). Copyright © 1982 by Thomas Nelson, Inc. Used by permission. All rights reserved.

Edited by Xulon Press.

Printed in the United States of America.

ISBN-13: 978-1-54565-621-1

TABLE OF CONTENTS

FOREWORD
by Nicole Victory

My mother has always been someone who finds happiness in her children. One of the things I remember most of my childhood is my mom carrying a huge JVC video camcorder around from place to place. The strap firmly placed on her shoulder, it was pleasantly used during holidays, concerts, field trips, birthday parties, days at home, summer afternoons, and feeding the ducks at our favorite park. She always seemed to find importance in the everyday, mundane moments of our comings and goings. Not only did she see those moments as important, but there was a sense of wanting to prolong and remember each detail and emotion. She has always been so good at celebrating her kids and believing the best in us.

Life has had its ups and downs throughout the years, but one consistent truth has been her love for us. It isn't a perfect love, but in it, I've always found comfort to be who I was created to be. I have asked my mom to release me time and again to adventure, missions, bravery, and failure. I've always had the personality to try the path less travelled…this, at times, has given her both grief and laughter. I love when my mom laughs at me. She has laughed at me my whole life, and she has loved me into becoming the brave woman I am today.

From her I learned the importance of our story and sharing it with others. I learned that it's okay to be scared—but it's never okay to bow down to the fear. And just like my mom has seen me grow up, I've seen her grow deeper. She has more patience, more kindness, been more loving, and shown more bravery than I could have ever imagined. I'm my mother's child in humor, looks, and valor. I see her in my cheeky moments, that I know come from the even deeper heritage of my pop. And I see her every time I choose forgiveness and mercy.

She has shown me what true reliance on God should look like and that prayer should be as normal as breathing. As you read this book you will see vulnerability and selflessness riddled through it. Whenever we choose these moments in our life, something beautiful is birthed. I believe in her, her story, and the impact it will have on you as the reader.

Now it's my turn to cheer her on.

–Nicole

Chapter 1

HERITAGE

*N*icole, my daughter, Is a story teller. She sometimes tells stories about my life to her friends, and sometimes even in front of audiences. Inevitably, she comes back and tells me about some of the impact the stories have on the people with whom she's shared. She shares with me about the tears some would shed and the joy they would experience as she narrates some of my story's…

As Nicole has gotten older, her interest in the happenings of my life has had a strange effect on me. I feel humbled that she so yearns to know so much about my life and the lessons I've learned. But I am also afraid to tell the whole story. After all, my life has not been easy. The lessons came at a great price.

For years she has been trying to get me to tell my story in my own words. Truth is, it never even dawned on me that I had a story worth telling. I figured it was just the hyperbole of an overly-loving daughter towards her mamma.

But then God started stirring something in me. As I look back over my life, I have come to realize that mine is a story of unconditional love. As it turns out, the love story I tried to write over and over again with the wrong men was already being written, but I was too blind to see that it was God who was the one always rescuing this damsel in distress. I was so busy pursuing life and trying to prove that I was strong, that it wasn't until much later that I learned the secret of forgiveness and how it is the key that gets us through our toughest times.

Some people say that hopelessness is attached to the circumstances around you. I have learned that hopelessness is a condition of the heart. At heart, I am a survivor. What and who I had to survive, I will tell you all about…later. But there is no doubt from where I got my survival instincts.

My father is the first born child of James Joseph Greene and Philomena Agatha Gushue-Greene.

They were married in January 1921 and my dad, John, was born on a cold September day of that same year, not a full nine months after they were wed. In those days, people in the small town of Quidi Vidi, St. John's, (in the province of Newfoundland, Canada) birthed their children in their homes with the help of midwives, a visiting doctor, and family members. The newlyweds were excited, but nervous, that their child seemed to be coming about a month early. But true to form, my dad was on his way and there was nothing anyone could do to stop him.

As the labor began, the joy and excitement turned into concern and worry. Something was wrong. Sensing it, my grandmother grabbed two hands full of blanket and pushed her firstborn into the world. "It's a boy," the doctor proclaimed. Philomena was exhausted but desperate to see her son. The second turned to minutes and they had not yet brought her son to her. She heard him cry. He sounded weak and small. She mustered all of her strength just to lift her head to catch a glimpse of her son. Her perfect son was as handsome as she always dreamed, but he was small. Tiny even. In fact, he was barely two pounds.

The doctor came to her and spoke the last words any new mother wants to hear.

"Your son will not survive the night. He is just too small. Say your prayers and say goodbye."

And just like that, their lives had changed, twice. First, they were parents of a newborn boy, their firstborn. There was such a thrill of love and hope when the doctor had announced it was a boy. There were even cheers. Then, just moments later, their boy, the one to carry their surname, the first to continue the family name, was given a death sentence.

Afraid and desperate, my grandparents cried out to God. And just as they finished praying, my grandmother declared with tears in her eyes, "My son will not die tonight!"

She picked him up and whispered into his ears, "You are a survivor. God gave you life for a reason. You are going to live!"

She carried the premature infant into the kitchen, as the blistering winds howled, rattling their small home that sat across from the boat docks in St. John. She swaddled him in a blanket and laid him in a bread pan and surrounded him with cotton. She then turned on the oven, opened the door and rested baby John on the door of the oven. It wasn't just the warmth and the heat of an oven that incubated him that night. It was the love and devotion of his parents who refused to accept what the doctor has said. My grandfather had to wake up early to work the next day. He pulled a chair next to his loving wife. The night was long and as they sat together, their young lives flashed before their eyes as they reminisced about happier times. Her piercing blue eyes filled with tears as she watched over her little baby. He held her hand for a moment just before going off to bed before having to wake up to go to work.

My grandmother was loving, unselfish, intelligent, and beautiful. She also happened to be a great chef. At a relatively young age, she landed a fancy chef position for one of the richest families in St. Johns. This particular family lived in a sprawling estate; they ran a corporation that owned the railway station. She was thrilled when this family hired her to cook all their meals. While most girls her age pined away, waiting for Mr. Wonderful to sweep them off of their feet, my independent grandmother was breaking the mold, making her own money, and trailblazing a path for women.

One day she heard about a dance that was happening down at Conception Bay Harbor. So she put on her best dress and went. All eyes were on the prettiest girl at the ball, including the eyes of young James—who was a hard-working young man looking to have a good time at the dance. It was love at first sight.

She was the best dancer he had ever seen and he knew that, the moment he saw her, he wanted to marry her. They met and they danced. They fell in love and became boyfriend and girlfriend. Young Philomena was so in love that she would ask her boyfriend to come to the fancy house where she would sneak him gourmet meals to eat. My grandfather would go on to say that he fell for her dancing but stayed for her cooking.

But all that was in the past. They had just made the decision, weeks prior, that she would quit her chef's job to raise their child. The very child they were trying to nurse through the night. The child they willed to stay alive. The child whose condition brought about the most heartfelt prayer they'd ever lifted up.

Needless to say, my father survived that fateful night. You might think I am referring to him when

I referenced that I got my survival skills from someone. Well, you'd be half right. I was actually referring to my grandmother.

Throughout my life, I can't recall the number of times my father told me that I am just like my grandmother. When I really think about it, that was probably the reason he favored me so and made me feel special my entire life.

I didn't set out to write this book to tell you about my grandmother's story. My plan was to share with you my story. But as it turns out, while diving into my story, I discovered several amazing people, A chief among them was this incredible woman that I never really even got to know and yet have a deeply personal relationship with. I knew her through my dad.

My grandmother is the example I would go on to live my life by. I can identify with her softer side as well as her sternness. But mostly, I learned that hopelessness may come to all of us but that's the time you have to decide what you are really made of. A situation like what happened with my father could have ruined that young couple's lives. But when you witness a miracle in the midst of your greatest storm, it's not the gloom and the fear you remember most. What sticks to you the most is the feeling you have the next morning when you realize that the baby they said was going to die is still alive!

There is nothing like staring hopelessness in the face and celebrating your victory over fear and doubt. You have been through your share of storms too, right? Your age, gender, religion, ethnicity…none of that keeps hopelessness from trying to sneak its way into your life.

I want to remind you that when you're facing a dire situation, an occasion where it looks like there is no way for a positive outcome, you have a choice. Like my grandmother did. You have a real choice. You can choose to believe the facts or you can believe the truth.

The facts say you are sick. But the truth says that by His stripes you are healed.

The facts say that everything has gone wrong and there is no way to turn things around. The truth says that all things work together for your good.

On September 12, 1921, a doctor stated what he thought was a fact. Based on all the information that was available to him, he said my dad wouldn't survive the first night of his life. But there was no way he could have predicted what love could do. As it turned out, love was stronger than facts. I want to let you know, dear reader, that not everything is as it may seem.

Hopelessness is a condition of the heart. There are days when waking up is the last thing you want to do. You wish you could just keep sleeping, forever. But there is good news. This good news was hard for me to see it at times because I wanted to call it quits on more than one occasion. But when I was at the very edge of despair, I would hear the voice of my grandmother in my spirit, "You are not going to die tonight!"

James and Philomena would go on to have seven other amazing children. The firstborn, John, lived through that fateful night and had a full life. He married and had six children. I am one of them. My grandmother's story had been written, mine is just beginning.

Chapter 2

THE EARLY YEARS

$\mathcal{M}$y dad enjoyed telling the story of the day he and my mom brought me home from the hospital as a newborn. We lived in a neighborhood called Stabb Court in St. John's in a row of identical-looking townhouses. All of the homes were constructed the same; half brick and half siding. Ours was lucky number thirteen.

My sister, who was only three-years old at the time, ran to the door as my dad carried me into the house. She jumped for joy and shouted with delight, "I have a baby, I have a baby!" Anyone that walked into the house thereafter was met by the same song and dance for months. "I have a baby upstairs," she would exclaim. I was her baby and she wanted everyone to know it.

No one's childhood is perfect and I am sure there were lots of bad things all around me growing up, but my parents did an amazing job of shielding me and preserving my innocence. I never knew what a slap from a man was…until I got married. Life, as a child, was idyllic in my little corner of the world.

My earliest memories involve all of us kids sitting around, in the living room, with dad in his favorite chair. We'd watch The Beverly Hillbillies and The Jackie Gleason show. My three brothers—Robert, Jimmy, and Eddy—are much older than I am. I also have two sisters: Agnes is three-years older than me and Lillian is my younger sister, who is six-years younger than me.

Dad's favorite chair had four skinny little legs, two wide armrests, and a small cushion. He loved sitting there with all of us lounging around our cozy living room.

My favorite times were when Humphrey Bogart was playing a gangster in a movie like *King of The Underworld,* or *Dead End,* because Bogart was Dad's favorite actor. After one of those movies, Dad would repeat lines from the movie and imitate Bogart as we all watched and laughed.

As with most things in my childhood, every-thing revolved around Dad. He was the life of every party. He had a way of making me feel special whenever I was around him.

We grew up Catholic and we went to church for all the important holidays. We were not allowed to eat breakfast before going to church. Being hungry in a place where the nuns were mean and the services were boring didn't make going to church an experience I grew to love. And to really seal the deal on my discontent with the church, one time I was even asked to leave the church by one of the stern nuns because my sister and I were giggling a little too loudly.

It is no wonder that I thought Jesus was a fairy tale, like Snow White or Cinderella. I was never taught about God, only religion.

When we would get home from church, we usually had a bologna, egg, and toast breakfast. On special occasions, Mom would make her famous *toutons,* served with molasses or maple syrup poured over them. Toutons are made from dough used for bread, except it is shaped like a giant pancake. They were, and continue to be, a Newfoundland favorite.

I got the same sense of family anytime my dad's family would visit from California or Halifax,

Nova Scotia. Most of Dad's siblings had moved away when I was a child, leaving just my dad and an aunt locally. Dad couldn't bring himself to leave his parents or his hometown. He was always overjoyed anytime his relatives would come to visit.

The extended family would usually come back home the first week of August for the yearly Royal St.John's Regatta—a tradition of 200 years held even unto today. With fantastic boat races, tents selling food, and goods as far as the eye could see, the regatta was like Christmas and Easter wrapped into one. My family from California even had their own tent set up where they sold hot dogs and french-fries.

The regatta was such a big deal at our house that Mom would take us shopping for new clothes for just that occasion.

There was such love and laughter in the air whenever we would all get together. If I close my eyes and concentrate really hard, I can still get a sense of security and the abundant feeling of family and love.

Even when Dad was surrounded by all of his family, he always looked for ways to make me feel special. Dad favored me. At times, when my mother would refuse something to me, he would override her and say something like, "Oh let her have it. It's not gonna hurt her."

He would bring me treats when he got home from work. He took me for walks. And for the first thirteen years of my life, he took such great care of me, there was no doubt of his love. He protected me, he gave me my own way, and he spoiled me with little things. I could not have asked for a better Dad.

I am sure my mother was always around too, but so many of my memories revolve around Dad in action while Mom was quietly cleaning, or cooking. She didn't seek attention or even seem to want any attention. She was content to let Dad run the show.

For instance, when I was six-years old and playing in the bathtub, I had created what I thought was the coolest hairstyle, using bubbles from shampoo. Curious to behold the masterpiece I'd created, I stood up on the edge of the bathtub to get a glimpse in the mirror, which was on the other side of the toilet. I didn't want to wet the hardwood floors, so I had to stretch and lean as I brought myself closer to the edge of the bathtub.

I was almost there, and thought that if I could just get on my tip-toes I would be able to see my shampoo creation. The beads of water were running down my leg and a puddle began to form around my feet. Undaunted, I lifted my tiny body onto my toes when, *whoops*, faster than I could even let out a scream, I fell toward the exposed bolt and screw that fastened the toilet to the floor.

Like a coconut being opened with a hammer, the screw opened a hole on the top of my head. And before I knew it, I was lying in a pool of warm blood. My older sister came running when she heard the loud thump. She ran into the bathroom and immediately cried out for Dad. He came rushing in. "Linda!" he almost whispered, as if he had lost his breathe, the moment he saw the tragic sight. With great concern towards me, he grabbed a towel to stop the steady stream of blood.

"You're going to be ay-okay, Linda," he reassured me as I moved in and out of consciousness.

Dad picked me up and ran to the phone. He didn't call the police, he didn't call for an ambulance, he called the one woman that he knew would know exactly what to do—his mother.

After he explained what happened, with a nervous stutter that I had never really noticed before, his mother called a cab and I was taken to the hospital. In all of the upheaval, it was always Dad who jumped into action. My mom was right there watching the events unfold and I know she was concerned about me, but Dad didn't consult her, he called his mom.

His mother was his go-to person, not my mother. I can't imagine what that must have done to her over the years. But growing up, it all felt normal. When you are a child, everything your parents do routinely becomes the norm.

I know now that it wasn't normal or healthy for a husband to always defer to his mother instead of his wife. Maybe that was one of the reasons there was such a quiet sadness in her eyes. Looking back, I can now see that mom must have struggled with depression. It wasn't something so commonly diagnosed back then. There weren't doctors that prescribed medicine for such a thing.

The clues are obvious now. When I think back to those years, Mom wasn't particularly maternal or nurturing. I know she loved us. Her way of expressing love was through performing her duties.

She kept a good house, she made sure everyone had enough to eat, and she made sure we had clean clothes to wear.

One time, when Mom worked an after-hours job cleaning a law office, she allowed my older sister and me to accompany her to work. We thought it was the coolest thing in the world to play with the fancy phones and spin around on the plush, leather chairs.

I remember watching her work. She didn't know I was watching. She was so dutiful and serious. It wasn't a fully-developed thought in my little mind, but I remember thinking that there was no joy in what she was doing. She wasn't mean or cold toward us. She just wasn't like my dad, who made everything fun and exciting.

Who could ever compete with the likes of him? He was larger than life. I can't say I grew up thinking that mom didn't love me. She certainly did. Maybe I didn't feel an absence of her affection because Dad loved us all enough for the both of them.

It didn't seem strange then but now I realize that Mom and Dad never owned a car. They really never even traveled to California to visit the family. I assume that Dad would much rather have spent any extra money he had on the family and having a good time than buying a car. We didn't find it too odd that we walked wherever we could or took a taxi everywhere else.

One time, on his payday, Dad invited me to go for a walk with him. We were going to his favorite bar, which was a thirty-minute walk down to Churchill Square, but I didn't care. It was the beginning of winter, but it wasn't cold out and the first snowfall had not arrived yet. Nothing could dampen my spirits. Not the long walk, not the chill in the air. Nothing! Because I got to spend time with Dad and he always, always got me treats.

Everywhere I went with him, he would hold my hand. As we walked, Dad told me some of his famous scary stories that he usually ended with a loud shout followed by a very self-indulgent laugh. He always managed to get a good jump and a scream out of me.

Our walk took us by the university where he worked as a custodian on the night shift. He told me about how he would sometimes take long breaks and eat all the ice cream one man could eat. I listened with wonder and thought to myself, "That must be a mountain of ice-cream!"

That day, Dad told me the story of the day he first saw Mom. He was going into a little corner market near Churchill Square. He was there running an errand for his mother. It was supposed to be another ordinary day. As he walked into the store, the attendant knew him by name and said *hello*. As he looked up to say *hello* back, he saw the most beautiful girl he had ever seen. She wore red lipstick, a red jacket, and stood at the checkout counter.

Red was such a bold and unusual color for a girl to be wearing in the middle of the day. It was as if everything in the store was in black and white and only she was in full technicolor. At that very moment, he fell in love with her. The girl with the red coat and the red lipstick.

Over the years, dad would repeat that story to me many times, but each time he would tell it he would get the same look in his eyes. The telling of that story always made him relive the joy of that moment.

I knew that we were getting close to his bar, because we always happened to stop in at his favorite little corner market. The people in the store knew him by name. Many years later I realized that the little store we frequented along our walks to the bar was the same store that he'd met Mom in.

Dad told me to choose any combination of candy, chips, and a soda. I felt like the most important person in his world to him. As we left the store, I remember him saying that he hoped to be home before the snowstorm came in. But I didn't think anything of it.

He took me by the hand again and lead me a little further down the road. He sat me on a bench overlooking the sometimes busy, but mostly quiet, square that was in front of the bar. He handed me my treats which always followed by his saying, "Linda, you sit right there and don't move until I come out!" He would say it uncharacteristically sternly so that I would listen. And I did listen.

I felt like such a big girl, sitting out there, enjoying my treats. I would watch the cars go by. People didn't even take a second look at the little girl sitting out in front of the bar. I thought to myself, well, if the adults all seem to think this is okay then it must be okay.

One hour turned to two hours and eventually, that familiar feeling would come back to me, reminding me that this was the part I didn't like.

Once all of the treats were finished and there were hardly any cars to look at, I was stuck outside of the bar waiting for my father to come out.

Every time the door opened, I hoped it was him. One time I was able to look inside as several people walked outside of the bar and I saw him sitting on a bar stool talking with people and everyone was laughing. It made me smile. He was having a good time! So I waited.

Just when I thought I was going to die of sheer boredom, the skies opened up and it began to snow. I loved the snow. So I played with the falling snow for a while and lost myself in it. So much so that I was sort of surprised when Dad stumbled out the door. He tried so hard to speak without slurring his speech. But there was little he could do to hide it. He was as drunk as I had ever seen him outside of the house.

Dad loved to drink. Some people say that alcohol magnifies your true personality. Some people get angry or feisty when they get drunk. Others cry and wallow in their sadness. But not my dad, he was a happy drunk. But a drunk is a drunk and his drinking was very hard for my mother to deal with.

When Dad really wanted to drink, he would have friends come to the house and they would make their own beer in the kitchen. He would drink so much that he would sometimes forget where he was.

As was the case when he stumbled out of the bar's door that day.

He took me by the hand and told me that it was time to go home. He began walking home, but as young as I was, I knew he was going the wrong way. I tried correcting him but he insisted he knew where he was going. After walking in the snow, in the wrong direction, for what seemed like forever—he realized he had gotten us lost. By this time, the snow was falling pretty hard. Dad was disoriented.

Looking back over moments like these over the course of my life, I see God's hand of protection over my life. Time and time again, God made a way out of dangerous situations I'd found myself in.

Miraculously, a taxi just happened to be driving by us and Dad was able to wave him down. Was it luck? Maybe! But I believe it was God looking out for me. And He did it time and time again. And I was going to need him more than ever in the years to come.

Just after my thirteenth birthday, my perfect and innocent childhood, that my parents worked so hard to protect, came crashing down. I had never known adversity. My dad was nearly perfect in my eyes. I thought we would always be the same perfect little family.

I was wrong. Mom and Dad were talking divorce.

Chapter 3

INNOCENCE LOST

It was a quiet Wednesday night. My sister and I were watching TV in the living room and mom was a bit more active than usual. Dad was at his night-shift job at the university. I thought nothing of it and kept watching TV.

A little while later, I looked up to see what Mom was up to again, and I noticed luggage being stacked near the door. I thought it was strange, but the innocence in me didn't even allow me to imagine what was happening. Mom was packing our bags and we were all leaving Dad. I had an older brother who lived there also, but he was hardly ever home. It would be as if Dad would be left all alone.

A few minutes later, Mom told us to shut the TV off and to get our shoes on. There was a determination in her voice which instantly broke us free from the trance the TV held on us. Before I knew it, we were leaving the only house I had ever known.

When I finally built up the nerve to say something to my mother, I asked her what was happening. And in her typical, non-emotional tone she said, "We are going to live with your aunt until we can get our own place!"

Reality was setting in as me and my two sisters walked behind her, toting our heavy luggage behind us as we walked towards the cab. My youngest sister, who was seven years old, did not really understand what was happening, but I was thirteen and my older sister was sixteen. We understood what was happening and we were heartbroken.

Tears started running down our faces. I thought, *Oh, my gosh, are we really leaving Dad behind?*

My mind began to flash back to the times that Mom would get angry at Dad for drinking too much. It was the only reason I remember hearing them argue. Well, she would get mad that he would spend so much money and get so drunk.

I recalled her saying to him, "I can't wait for these kids to be grown so that I can leave this house and you!" But none of us ever thought she would actually do it. Especially Dad!

The walk took forever, as with each step I felt further and further away from my poor old Dad. It was torturous. How could I live without him?

We had finally arrived at my aunt's house. I used to love visiting her because she was always so kind and fun. We got along great with her children, our cousins. We exchanged pleasantries, we were shown to our room, and before long everyone was acting like everything was just fine.

I now know that what I had been witness to, was the bravest moment of my mom's life. It must have taken such courage to call it *done* and walk away from him. I was too busy worrying about my dad at the moment, but I can now appreciate the inner strength and fortitude she had to muster up to be able to walk away. After all, no one gets married to get divorced.

All I could think of was how my dad must have reacted when he walked into our house after his long shift, to find the house empty. How he must have walked into his bedroom to see the closets and bureaus empty. He must have called out to us when he didn't see his daughters in our rooms.

The next day, Dad made his way over to my aunt's house. He came to fight for his family. Initially I thought he was romantic and even heroic the way he came to fight for us. But then I heard Mom accuse him of being drunk. He was!

For two days he kept calling my aunt's house to try to persuade Mom to come back home, but each time, he was drunk. He was saying all the right things, but his words were being drowned out by his actions. I heard Mom tell him that if he really wanted us back, he would stop drinking.

Dad was trapped between his love for his family and his addiction to alcohol. He promised to change if we would just come home, but his actions were sending Mom a different message. The drinking had become too much for her to handle. She had made up her mind. The marriage was over.

Dad never gave up trying. Mom told him that there was nothing that he could do or say to get her back home. Dejected and defeated, he asked to talk to me and my older sister.

It was the first time in a few days that we'd gotten to talk to him. The moment I heard his voice, tears gushed from my eyes, down my checks and started forming a puddle on the kitchen table, where I was sitting. He sounded so beaten and tired.

He asked us to come home. He told us that he couldn't live without us. His cry was so heart-breaking. He told us that he'd lost our mom and maybe there was nothing he could do about that, but he didn't want to lose us, too.

I'll never forget what Dad said that made me agree to come home. It wasn't just what he said but there was a tone in his voice that I had never heard before. He told us that he didn't know what would become of him that night if we didn't agree to come home. There was such a tragic desper-ation in his words. He was begging us to come home and, as pathetic as it all might seem now, at least he expressed emotion and demonstrated something that resembled love towards us.

As usual, there was such a stark contrast between Mom and Dad. He passionately, albeit drunkenly, fought for my sister and I while I got the distinct impression that Mom only had us with her out of some motherly obligation to raise us until we could be on our own. She wasn't built like other moms. Sadly, the nurturing gene that most Moms of that era had, my mom never had. I felt she was indifferent towards us.

Then there was Dad. The crying had escalated as he pleaded over the phone for my sister and I to come home. The only other time I had ever heard dad cry like that was when his beloved mother passed away. I never wanted to hear that sound again, but here it was. Crying for me and my sister the way he cried after losing his mom. Daughters are not designed to ignore their father's cries. Can you imagine? The man I grew up needing all of my life was now telling me how much he needed me.

My sister and I talked it over with each other and we immediately agreed that we had no choice but to go back to live with Dad.

When Mom heard that we had decided to go back with Dad, she simply said, "If you want to go back to him, go ahead." As characteristically laid back and detached as ever.

Even though we had only been staying at my aunt's house for a couple of days, it was a nice time. There was also more family, more things to do, and more people to play with. But the decision had been made.

An unintended consequence from choosing to go back with Dad was that my older sister and I had to walk out on our little sister, who had to stay with our mom . We used to play dress up with her and treated her like a doll. Walking away from her was harder than walking away from Mom.

We got back on the phone and told Dad we were coming home, and the cries instantly turned into laughter, and the desperation turned to gratitude. He couldn't believe it. He was elated. I could never put into words the exact feeling I felt listening to that amazing transition in him. It was as if someone flipped a switch in his heart and he could be happy again.

The next day we walked back home. Dad wasn't a man that was overly emotional or expressive with things, only when he was having a few beers . He was usually a pleasant, happy person. But that day, he was full of joy. His girls were back home. I remember coming home to find some of my favorite treats and little presents. He must have gone out just to show his appreciation to us for coming home.

For the first few days we were all a bit awkward. Life without Mom was difficult at first. Not only did we miss her presence, but now we had to do a lot of the things she did for us that we had taken for granted. There was no one there to keep the house and take care of Dad, so we had to do it. It was quite a change and it took some getting used to.

With each passing week, we became more and more aware of what it meant to live with just my dad. Because Mom still wasn't there, we had to do the chores she'd done.

I found myself resenting Mom. I knew that it was my decision to come back to live with Dad, but that didn't keep me from feeling abandoned by her. She could have come home any time she wanted. God knows Dad would have taken her back. In fact, there were weeks where Dad tried to drink less and to make more of an effort to persuade Mom to come home. But he was met with disdain and rejection. The love was gone!

They say that perception is truth and, at thirteen, I just wasn't able to separate truth from my perception. Mom didn't leave me. She left Dad. But I felt like she abandoned the family. I felt like she was being selfish. I thought that if she would have loved us enough, she would have come home, but she never did. These were the seeds of resentment I would carry for years to come.

I wanted to force her to keep our family together and, when she didn't respond, I found myself trying to punish her in my own little ways.

I started doing things that she never allowed us to do in the house. I started eating in the living room—she would never have allowed that. I started leaving the dishes on the table until the next day. Then my attitude escalated to staying up late at night and talking on the phone with my friends well after bedtime.

Day after day, I kept expecting someone to tell me that I was being a bad girl. I was waiting for someone to scold me or punish me, but all of a sudden there was no one to enforce the rules of proper conduct.

Dad started to notice that my sister and I were straying from what he considered to be our normal behavior, so he asked his father to come stay with us while he was at work. But it was too late. My sister and I had already tasted a little bit of freedom and we liked it. We wanted more! So, we appeased Dad and Granddad just long enough so that they both thought that we didn't need the extra supervision.

I started skipping school and hanging out with my friends. We would smoke, listen to music, walk around…basically anything we could do to kill time as long as it wasn't school.

My best days were Fridays, because that is when we would go to clubs or parties. I hung out with people that were a few years older than me and I supposed that helped me look a little older, because I didn't seem to have any trouble getting into clubs.

I wasn't interested in boys at the time. All I wanted to do was dance with my friends and have a good time. Everything changed one Friday night when a boy named Harry asked me to dance. I knew him socially, but we had never said a word to each other. All my girlfriends swooned whenever they saw him. They all had a crush on him. That part of my development had not yet happened, but everything was about to change for me.

I had noticed him looking in my direction for about an hour. I didn't really think anything of it. Maybe he was looking at one of my friends. I never even dreamt of the possibility that it was me he was looking at.

After dancing a few songs with my girlfriend's, my eyes just automatically looked for him in the crowd. I just wanted to see his face again. He was so cute.

Then someone called my name. When I turned to respond, Harry was right behind me. He was standing there in all his glory. His blond hair was almost glowing from the club lights and his eyes were like the blue of the ocean.

I stumbled on my words and, before I could say anything, he asked me to dance. He took my hand and walked me to the dance floor. I turned to look at my friends and they were all standing there in amazement, with the biggest smiles on their faces, silently telling me to go for it.

The music was loud. Everyone was dancing and bumping into one another. I decided to do what my friends told me to do: go for it. And so we danced. One song, then another, and before I knew it, we'd danced the entire night. He was so attentive to me. For the first time ever, I could tell that a boy really liked me and it made me feel so special.

It was the end of the night and everyone was getting ready to go home. I had never been in a situation like this. I didn't know what to do with these strange new feelings I was experiencing. It was really like having butterflies in my belly.

We said good night and we just looked at each other for what felt like an eternity. Was this to be my first real kiss?

Just then, he took my hand and pulled me into him. This was it! So I closed my eyes and puckered up. We kissed. I kept my eyes closed even after it was over, for just another second. I wanted to remember every detail of that experience.

I opened my eyes to Harry's sweet smile as he turned and walked away. It was the perfect first kiss…but I never saw Harry again after that. I heard later that his family moved away.

Chapter 9

IN THE REAL WORLD

*I*t was a warm summer day and my girlfriends and I were hanging out on my front steps as we did on a regular basis. We heard the sound of a motorcycle coming up the street and we all looked up to watch. The person riding noticed us looking at him, so he boldly pulled over and said *hello*. He was ruggedly handsome and had a friendly smile. We all became instant friends.

His name was William and, for the following two months, he would drop by at least once a week. It became something we all looked forward to.

On one of his unannounced visits, he asked me if I wanted to go for a ride with him. I wanted to say *yes*, but I was frightened at first. It didn't take a lot of convincing before I was on the back of his bike though, feeling the wind in my hair, holding on to this familiar stranger who really seemed to like me. I liked him too.

Falling in love is like a wild roller coaster. At fourteen, puppy love feels like the real thing. Falling in love with William was a wild new experience for me. I could not possibly know what the future held for me with William but, at that moment, I was happy!

Other than the love I had received from my dad and my siblings, I had never known love from someone outside of my family. This other form of love was something new and it captured me completely.

My relationship with my dad had changed. His drinking had gotten worse. Although he never stopped loving me, he seemed to stop *caring* for me. In fact, it became my job to care for him. The roles had shifted. He was still my dad and I always gave him that place of respect. It is natural for aging parents to depend more on their children. But this was happening too soon. Ready or not, I had to grow up.

At fourteen, I remember asking myself who the parent was, him or me? We still had our moments of fun and closeness but after Mom left, things just weren't the same between us.

That left an emptiness in my heart that William began to fill. Will was three years older than me but no one seemed to care too much about our age difference. Dad seemed to like him and they would sometimes drink together.

We spent every day together once we started dating. It was like he was becoming part of my family and it was perfect.

After meeting his parents and siblings, our relationship moved into high gear. This rollercoaster of a love story was everything I could have asked for.

His mother accepted me instantly. At first, I didn't know how to respond to her affection and kindness. She was the polar opposite of my mother in that she was expressive with her words and very generous with her affection. In no time I considered her to be a second mother to me and I become like another daughter to her.

I'll never forget the first time she told me she loved me. Will and I were leaving the house to grab a bite to eat and she just said it, "I Love You, Linda!"

I tried to play it cool but in reality those words released a flood of emotions that were locked deep within. I said it back, "I love you, too!"

My eyes welled up with tears that I tried to brush away so that no one else would notice. In that house, that was a common thing they said to one another. It was a kindness I would never ever forget. From that moment on, I could say *I love you* and hear it back!

William's mom was very involved with the Salvation Army. She was a high-ranking minister, though her husband wasn't as involved. She used to tell me that she was praying for me and that made me feel good.

She got me to visit the Salvation Army a few times. I actually loved the music and the people were friendly. It was a far cry from the mean nuns and the boring Masses at my parents' church.

This church was alive and friendly. I wasn't fully convinced that Jesus loved me, but for the first time I could feel like someone who said they loved Jesus also loved me.

Will's dad and siblings were equally generous with their affections. They had all adopted me as another family member and often chose my side when Will and I would have little disagreements. I was a part of a loving family.

William became my everything. We did everything together and we went almost everywhere together. I would do anything to keep him in my life.

Things were moving fast. We partied on the weekends and hung out during the week. We both enjoyed dancing drinking and smoking . Life was spinning faster and faster. Way too fast for a fourteen-year old girl to keep up with.

I started to find myself in situations that were way over my head, specifically with other boys. I began to realize the effect I had on some boys. I felt their eyes on me when I moved around the club, even when I was dancing with William.

One night at the club, I was on my way to the bathroom when I recognized one of William's relatives walking in front of me. We said hello and continued our walk to the bathroom.

When we got close, he grabbed me and pulled me into the boys' bathroom. He pushed me up against the wall and started trying to kiss me as his hands were trying to get inside my clothes. I was in total shock. I was acting on instinct as I tried to fight him off of me, but it was as if everything was moving in slow motion. Every second felt like a minute.

His strength seemed to increase as I no longer had the ability to fight him off. I was at his mercy. I was helpless. I thought he was going to rape me.

I began to cry and begged him to stop. He said cruel things to me. He told me that William wasn't the only family member worthy of my affection and that if I was really nice, I would share myself with him too.

In that moment of pure fear, I began to ask God to help me. Not in any specific words. It was just a desperation in my soul that began to cry out. Help Me! Somebody Help Me!

He had pinned my arms behind my back with one hand and he had lifted my skirt with his other hand when, at that very moment, someone walked in. The stranger looked at me and asked me if I was okay. I wasn't. And just like that, he released me.

I ran out of that bathroom and into the arms of one of my best friends. I made it out of that bathroom, but a left a piece of my innocence in there. I knew for myself how evil men could be now and it left me terrified.

I told my friend what happened but I made her promise never to tell William. I thought he wouldn't understand. I was afraid he would blame me for not stopping him sooner, for not being stronger, for letting him touch me. I couldn't risk losing William's love.

I've often wondered what would have happened if that stranger hadn't walked into that bathroom right when he did. I also wondered if God heard the prayer of desperation from my soul that night.

Over the years, I have heard stories of angels among us that have helped regular people get out of extraordinary situations. I like to think that maybe I was saved by an angel that night. I don't know if he was a celestial being, but he was definitely my guardian that night.

Life wasn't slowing down for me. That very same year, two of my girlfriends and I decided that we wanted to go to a park that was about three miles away. It would take us about an hour to walk there or maybe we could hitch a ride. So off we went.

About twenty minutes into our walk, we managed to hitch a ride with a couple of young guys who said they were going to the same park. We had never seen them before but they seemed like really nice guys, so we all got in.

The driver took a turn away from the park that we wanted to go to. Instead they offered to take us to have a picnic and to have a few beers. I did not want to go but I was outvoted by my other two single girlfriends who clearly didn't mind the attention those boys were giving them.

They were joking and making us laugh. It seemed harmless. They parked the car and there was a nervous energy all around. Electricity was sparking between the boy in the back and one of my friends. I was riding in the front with the driver.

The entire back seat decided to go for a walk to sightsee and before I knew it, I was alone with the driver. He had such a nice smile and reminded me of one of my brothers. It seemed harmless, but in the back of my mind, I remained cautious. The bathroom incident made me look at every man with a bit of suspicion.

After about an hour of chatting and sipping on a few beers, the driver began getting a little flirty with me. I had already told him about William and how much I loved him, so I was able to deflect any and all verbal attempts to get my attention.

Another hour went by and I began to wonder where my friends were and what was taking so long. My driver friend had polished off a six pack all by himself and he didn't seem to be the same person who was making all those jokes only a few hours earlier.

I recognized the look in his eyes. I told him that I was getting worried about my friends and that we should go look for them. As I went to open the door, he pounced on me like a lion on his prey.

In shock, I couldn't believe this was happening to me *again*. He forcefully tried to kiss me. I tried avoiding his lips. He was strong! Much stronger than me.

I was wearing shorts and a halter top. His hands were frantically trying to remove my clothes while I frantically fought to keep them on.

Repeatedly, I tried to push him away. It felt so familiar. But this time, there was no angel that was going to walk in to save me. I was on my own. Crying out to God wouldn't do me any good. So I just cried.

A dark realization had come over me. This strange man who was much stronger than me was going to rape me and there was nothing I could do about it. That deeply disturbing truth brought forth a type of cry in me that I had never released.

I begged him to stop. I cried out, "Please, don't do this to me!" as my weeping drowned out the words trying to come out of my mouth.

He was not in control of himself. The drink and the desire to be satisfied had overtaken whatever decency may have ever existed in him. He wasn't a man at that moment, he was an animal.

In sheer desperation, I began to shriek and scream, "Somebody help me!" as loud as I could.

I was still pure. William and I had talked about maybe one day getting intimate. But there I was with this total stranger and he was going to take the gift I could only give away once and to only one person. I did not want that to be him, I wanted it to be William.

And for no apparent reason, he just stopped his attack on me. He looked at me and said. "You big sook (cry baby) go on with your stupid friends. Go home to your mommy!"

He released me and I ran out of the car as he drove off leaving us all behind. I only told my best friend, who later emerged from her walk to find me crying with my clothes half torn.

We walked back home and never talked about it again. The shame that this happened twice was more than I could ever come to terms with. I am not sure how or why, but I somehow blamed myself, not the driver and not William's relative who tried to take advantage of me in the bathroom.

In the #Me Too era we are living in now, women are being empowered to tell their stories. Maybe it has given me the courage I needed to tell mine, because now that I am grown I know some things that I wish I'd known back then.

- I now know that it wasn't my fault. I didn't do anything to provoke or to deserve what those men did to me when I was just a child. How I dressed or the way I smelled did not give them the right to attack me. They were to blame, not me!

- I was too young and innocent to say anything to them back then but I am a different person now.

- If I could go back and confront them, I would say, "Shame on you! You tried to force yourself on a child. It doesn't matter how old I looked, I was only fourteen.

- You may not have gotten what you wanted out of me but you took away something I desperately needed. I wasn't ready to lose my innocence. And you stripped it away from me. I wasn't ready to lose faith in people, specifically men, and you impaired my ability to trust men. I carried the scars you gave me for a long time. For years, I was deficient in the area of intimacy."

- I now know that I should have said something to the people who love me. I should have told my dad. He would have fought for me. I should have told William and given him a chance to be the man I hoped he was. I should have told William's mom. She would have known what to do.

By keeping my mouth shut, I let them get away with what they did to me. I shudder to think of how many other girls may have had to suffer what I endured because I was too scared to say anything. I should have said something to someone!

- I now know that I am stronger than my attackers thought I was. My tears turned into weapons against you and my weakness became a strength. You tried to break my spirit and take my purity, but you couldn't. In the end, I was stronger.

This wouldn't be the only time I would be attacked. But I learned something about myself. I am strong.

- I now know that Jesus heals even your most serious wounds. Later in this book, I will share how I came to know Jesus and what a difference He has made in my life. But if you only read this section, I can't wait until then to tell you this good news.

If you have ever been hurt or abused, there is healing when you enter into a personal relationship with Jesus. You can get to know God through Jesus. He will then help you heal from your past. He then will help you discover your purpose so that you can make a difference in the world.

It is never too late to tell your story. Look at me. I am telling mine forty-five years after it happened. There is no statute of limitations on your ability to tell your story.

Chapter 5

A FLASH OF LIGHT

My relationship with William had blossomed. I experienced a lot of "firsts" with him. He was the first boy I had ever introduced to my family. He was the first boy I ever loved. He was the first boy to ever spend the night at my house, which also means that he was the first boy I ever slept with.

I was happy. It was like playing house. Dad had even gotten me a part-time job as a cashier at the university's cafe. So, my days were filled with going to school, going to work, then coming home to Dad and, often times, William.

Those two got along a little too well, especially on the weekends after payday. They would drink. Even though I was often present, I never drank with Dad. It was just one of those things that I never felt comfortable doing.

In the beginning, William and I hardly ever got into fights even though I felt like he was starting to take me for granted. Besides drinking a little too much with my father, William would sometimes leave the house for days at a time. Each time he came back home, he was a little less sincere with his apologies.

After a few months of William essentially living with dad and me, I noticed that my menstrual cycle was a bit late. I thought it was a little strange but didn't pay it too much attention to it. It wasn't too rare an occurrence that I would be a week or two late.

A few weeks later I decided to do the math and I discovered that my period was more than two months late. I tried to remain calm.

I made an appointment to see my doctor. Back in those days, they didn't sell over-the-counter pregnancy tests where I lived. So I went to my doctor's private practice and they ran some tests. I waited and waited for the results. I couldn't help but daydream about what it would be like to have a baby. I had never really given it much thought. I was only fifteen. But now that I knew sitting there in that doctor's office, becoming a mom was a real possibility, I could feel a change happening inside of me.

When my doctor returned, I could tell she had news for me by the look on her face. Before she could even speak I blurted out, "I'm pregnant, right?" She sighed heavy and confirmed it. I could tell that she was worried about me, being that I was so young.

Fear was my first reaction. How was I going to take care of this baby? What are people going to think of me? I hope William is happy. Maybe becoming a dad will help settle him down a bit. The future was so uncertain at that moment.

But at the same time, deep inside there was an unspeakable joy brewing in me. I was afraid to show what I was feeling inside. I know I was supposed to feel ashamed, and part of me was. But I was going to have a baby. I thought about how much fun it was when I'd taken care of my sister, who was six years younger than me. I could only imagine what it would be like having my own baby.

When I got home from the doctor's visit, I had to wait for William to get back from work. Different scenarios were playing in my mind where, in most of them, William and I became a real family. I was scared…but excited.

When William finally got home, I could hardly wait for him to walk through the door. I ran towards him and told him I had the most exciting news to tell him. He smiled at me as my excitement began to rub off on him.

I took his hand and placed it on my belly, I looked him in the eyes and said, "We are going to have a baby!"

He smiled so big as tears of joy began to stream down my cheeks. He picked me up and spun me around.

A few nights later, William and Dad were at it again. They were three sheets to the wind when William told me that he wanted to tell my dad the good news. I wasn't scared that Dad would be angry. At this point, I felt like he would be all right with just about anything. But still, I was nervous.

William said, "Mr. Greene, we have some big news to share with you." Dad smiled at us as his face lit up with expectation. "What is it?" he asked.

"You are going to be a granddad!" William exclaimed with joy.

The excitement on Dad's face changed to shock. A sadness fell over Dad's eyes. He took a huge swig of beer and swallowed deep. "I knew this would happen!" He said shaking his head. Then, he looked at me so tenderly and said, "A baby having a baby!"

I put my head down in shame as I heard him take another sip of beer. I looked up at him His bottom lip quivered as he fought to keep his emotions inside only because he was worried about me.

I replied, "We are going to be a family, Dad."

He filled his mouth full with the last of his beer. He laid the bottle down gently on the table and quietly said, "Okay, Linda, okay!" Then he walked into the other room.

I didn't really understand his reaction at the time and we never spoke about it afterwards. But it was as if Dad knew at that moment what hardship was waiting for me in the road ahead. He somehow looked into my future and caught a glimpse of how hard it would be for me to raise my child, and it brought him profound sadness, not for himself, but for me.

I was undaunted. Dad would have my back. He always did.

William, on the other hand, did not settle down. His drinking got worse and he began to spend more time out of the house. I had not even had the baby yet when I began to realize that William was not going to be a good father. He certainly turned out to be a disappointment as a boyfriend. He played games with my emotions. One day he would tell me he loved me and the next day he would disappear for three days and act indifferent about my feelings when he would come home.

The first time he pushed me, we were arguing about his drinking and about how much money he was spending. We had gotten into a few arguments about this in the past, but this time I was a bit more persistent about making my point. I tried to wake him up to the reality that he was going to be a dad and that he had to change his ways.

He wanted to leave the house but I got in his way asking him not to go. I asked him to stay and talk it out. In a fit of rage, he grabbed me by the shoulders and shoved me down to the ground—with no regard for our baby.

I wasn't so upset that he'd shoved me. I blamed myself for making him angry. But what really hurt me was that William didn't think twice about the baby growing in my belly.

The first time William hit me was the night I took him to the company Christmas party. I was excited to get all dressed up and to see him looking so handsome, it made me so happy. The evening started off perfectly. We held hands as we walked into the party and I had this fleeting moment where I thought everything would be fine between us. I looked around and saw all the other couples having a good time and felt like Will and I would fit right in.

Midway through the party, I noticed William getting very friendly with one of my friends. She was pretty and didn't seem to notice how this was affecting me. They were flirting with each other. I knew that they both had a little too much to drink and so I tried to ignore what was happening.

I went up to William and took him to the dance floor. We always enjoyed dancing together. The music was loud and the atmosphere was electric. I closed my eyes for a moment as we danced. I was trying so hard to make this night something special.

When the song ended we went back to the table with all of our friends and, within minutes, William's attention was right back on my friend.

I took my things and started heading toward the door. I was expecting for William to run after me and ask me to stay or offer to leave with me. As I approached the doors, I turned around to see if William was coming after me. To my horror, he and she were on the dance floor. He was dancing with her the way he'd danced with me.

It was a fifteen-minute walk home and I was fuming the entire way.

I was in bed when I heard William stumble into the room. He was drunk. I acted like I was asleep. I was angry but I knew that talking to him while he was still drunk would have been a big waste of time.

He slipped into bed, and to my amazement, he tried to get fresh with me. I was so offended. My friend must not have given him what he wanted now he was going to get it from me? I don't think so!

I shouted at him and told him to go to sleep. I told him how his actions at the party made me feel betrayed and hurt. But my anger didn't change a thing in him he even got more aggressive . He began forcing himself on me.

Old feelings of fear and panic rushed in, but this was different. This was on my home. I had more control, or so I thought.

I pushed him off me and I told him, "I am nobody's second choice! Get off me right now!" I felt strong and was proud of myself for standing up to him.

Then, without any warning, I saw the look of rage come over him. He clinched his fist and held it over me for a split second. Before I could even react, he thrusted his fist towards my face and punched me right between the eyes, on the bridge of my nose.

I saw a flash of light in the darkness of the room. There was an instant gush of blood flowing from my nose. My vision was blurry and I pushed him off of me and ran to the bathroom. I tried not to make a lot of noise because I didn't want William to get in trouble with Dad.

I told myself that the relationship was over. How could I ever love someone that would hurt me like that? As I cleaned myself up and managed to stop the blood flow, I prepared a speech for him. Who did he think he was to just hit me and think nothing would change?

I went back in the room with guns ablaze. And as I began my prepared statements, I noticed he was knocked out cold. He just lay there on the bed...

passed out. My pillow was still covered with blood and William on his side of the bed, sound asleep.

In the morning, he convinced me that everything that happened that night was my fault. He told me that he felt rejected at the party when I left him there all alone. Then he became even more angry when he tried to make love to the woman he loves and I cruelly rejected him. Then he told me that he meant to punch the pillow and that my face just got in the way.

Every time we got into a fight, he would tell me that I had provoked him. He was so convincing that I would end up actually believing that it was my fault that he had to hit me. He made me believe that if I was nicer to him and didn't instigate him to lose his temper, he would never, ever harm me. It was my fault that he would shove me to the ground. He made me believe that I had it coming, but that I could prevent it if only I would listen to him, or get out of his way, or simply shut my mouth.

I ended up feeling sorry for him. I believed that he never really intended to hurt me. I had to do better so that he could love me the way he wanted to love me.

My eyes were swollen that next morning. I concealed my injuries from my dad by wearing makeup, styling my hair a little differently, and wearing glasses. Dad never noticed what William was doing to me.

Chapter 6

LOVE AT FIRST SIGHT

*O*ver the next few months, William and I broke up several times. My self-esteem was so low and deflated. Every time I tried to leave him, he would say something to make me feel like I could never break free from our toxic relationship.

He only talked lovingly about our child when it helped get him something he wanted or when I was at my breaking point. He knew how badly I wanted for us to be a family.

He used it to his advantage. Will also knew that I didn't want our son to grow up without his father at home.

Like it or not, I was stuck with William in my life. That is what I believed.

Plus, it wasn't all bad. There were some good days in between the bad days.

We routinely went to the movie theater together. That was one of my favorite things to do with William. The fresh popcorn and the thrill of a newly-released film felt like a mini-adventure for us.

We also went out to eat at different restaurants. On those days, we felt like we were a normal family. When things were good, I could see ourselves raising our child together and being in love.

William would sometimes buy me flowers and surprise me for no specific reason. The man was totally capable of being charming and irresistible. I later learned that flowers don't always mean *I Love You*.

My favorite things to do with William was to hang out at his house with his family. I felt loved and safe there. His mother and siblings had accepted us as a part of their family.

I remember the feeling of family that would cover me like a warm blanket when we would all sit around the dinner table and enjoy one another's conversation and company. Those were the moments that gave me hope that William could change. When I considered the type of home life he enjoyed, there was reason to be hopeful.

People wonder how abused people can stay in relationships that are obviously toxic and bad for their health. Looking back now, I can honestly say that some of the reasons for staying sounded logical to me at the time. I felt my child deserved to be raised by both of his parents. I believed that if I could change, William could change too. I looked at the great family he came from and I wanted to create that with him.

I had finally mustered up the courage to visit Mom and break the big news to her. As I approached the door to her apartment, I could smell the homemade fishcakes she was cooking. I knocked on the door and waited to see if she would react to my baby bump.

True to form, mom simply looked at my belly and asked, "How far along are you?" without any emotion whatsoever. I was five-months pregnant.

Then she asked, "Are you staying with your dad?" I told her I had no place else to go and that I was fine at Dad's house. We ate some food and that was that.

When I got pregnant, there was an instant change in my life. I no longer had a desire to hang out with my friends, much less drink or go to clubs.

I didn't even miss it. I was so focused on starting a family that I decided to drop out of school and pick up more hours at the university. It seemed like the logical thing to do at that time. I did go back ten years later to finish my education.

William worked the same hours I did, so we didn't see each other during the day. He was drinking almost every night with Dad and, when he wasn't drinking at home, he was out with his friends. I was home alone…a lot. I was lonely.

We fought more frequently and our fights almost always ended with him pushing me around. Every time he would shake me violently and throw me around I would get tiny flashbacks of those horrific moments that those men tried to have their way with me, in years prior. I would sometimes be paralyzed with fear. I didn't know how to speak up or even defend myself.

I thought I was supposed to just keep forgiving him because that is what you do when you love someone. All I had going for me was my baby.

Fortunately, I never experienced morning sickness or any of the other things some young mothers have to suffer through. I found pregnancy to be easy. Life with William was the difficult part.

Right around the time of my due date, I had a scheduled appointment at my doctor's office. It was about a thirty-minute walk and I made it easily. After she examined me, she informed me that I was in labor. She instructed me to go home, get my things, and meet her at the hospital.

She didn't know I had walked there so I just walked back home. Dad was there when I got home and he immediately called a cab. He got in the cab with me and never left my side.

William was nowhere to be found.

My father was the only person allowed in my room as they prepared me to deliver the baby. He looked so funny dressed up in the gown and mask they gave him. He did everything he could to keep me calm and entertained while we waited.

William's mother, sister and my sister were in the waiting room and Dad would come in and tell me how excited they were to meet the baby.

No one else was allowed in during the actual labor which lasted a grueling sixteen hours. I was in a Catholic hospital and I had never had a good experience with a single nun. And why should this experience be any different?

I politely called one of the nurses, who was a nun, and asked her for something to ease the pain. She firmly told me, "Every mother must suffer as they bring their child into this world!"

So, with no medication and sixteen long hours of excruciating pain, the baby was finally here. I waited with bated breath to hear the cry and, after just a few seconds of delivery, I heard a strong cry.

"It's a boy!" the doctor announced. They cleaned him up and brought him over to me and put him on my chest. He was so little and perfect. Amazingly, he lifted his tiny head and looked right at me. It was love at first sight.

He weighed five pounds and thirteen ounces. I named him Wilson. William never even bothered showing up at the hospital that day.

The next day I went to feed my son in the nursery. In those days, you had to visit your baby at the nursery. When I came back to my room, there was a woman with a briefcase sitting next to my bed waiting for me. She was in her mid-fifties and she was well dressed.

She started talking about my baby and asked how he was doing. She then asked how I was feeling. Then she asked me if I had ever considered giving my son up for adoption.

Abortion was never something I thought about and no one ever even proposed such a thing to me. But now, after my son was born, I found it so humiliating and insulting for someone to ask me this.

I defiantly told her that I would never give my child up. She persisted and told me to think about it. I was barely sixteen years old and she mentioned that maybe it would be better for my son to have a stable home with a married couple to raise him.

I knew I was young and I realized that there were other people that could give my son more material things than I could at that time, but no one was going to love him like his momma would love him. Even the thought of it broke my heart into pieces.

I thanked her for her visit and then insisted that she leave me and my son alone, forever.

Just as she was leaving, my dad walked into the room and asked me what that was all about. With tears in my eyes I filled him in on everything she had said, he walked over to the door and spoke in a loud voice, "that woman better not come back here again," just loud enough that I think she heard him.

Two days later, William finally came to meet his son. He was never going to be the dad I hoped he would be but that didn't keep me from feeling excited when he showed up. We walked down to the nursery together and I pointed him out to his father. William was genuinely happy to see his son. And for a moment, I allowed myself to believe that everything was going to be better now.

I stayed at the hospital for an entire week. Within hours, William had disappeared. It was Dad who helped with the baby who was sometimes colicky, crying for hours at a time.

As I watched my relationship with William fall apart, my relationship with my daddy was stronger than ever.

He wasn't overly expressive about his feelings, but he was there for us each and every day.

Chapter 7

WEDDING BELLS & BRUISES

*T*he mind is a powerful thing. You can convince yourself of almost anything with a little help from the people around you. I was convinced that I was trapped in my relationship with William. My low self-esteem helped William convince me that no one else would ever love me and that he was the only man that would.

Our son was a year old when we decided to move into our own place. I believed it was a good idea. I thought that being in our own apartment would help us feel more like a family unit. Even though I cherished the help we received from Dad and some of his family, I wanted to try doing it on our own. We weren't making a lot of money at the time, but we were making enough money to afford our own place and pay our own bills. We were even able to get our own car. Life felt like it was starting to come together. I was driven by my desire to give my son a place to grow up in and call home.

I was almost seventeen now but I felt a lot older on the inside. I thought I really loved William. Abused people don't only stay in the relationship out of fear, they sometimes stay out of a messed up idea of what love is. People on the outside can see it for the dysfunction that it is, but not the person enduring the pain. They are made to believe that their very survival depends on their ability to make the best of things.

Two years later, we got married.

Yes, I married William! Each milestone we celebrated was embedded with empty promises and meaningless gestures that I interpreted for kindness and affection.

I had such high hopes that William would develop into the father our son deserved. But in reality, he didn't help raise our son. He never seemed to connect with him.

Although Will would go weeks and months with good behavior, trying to prove he could change, eventually he always reverted to the same old drinking and running around for days at a time.

All of my wishful thinking never produced change. Things don't just change because you want them to. Having our son, getting our own apartment, getting married; none of those things changed the sad reality of our relationship. I realize now that God had placed people in our lives that could have really helped us change if we had only accepted it. We needed God but I felt like I didn't know how to find Him.

I am only able to tell this story because of God's divine protection and His providential care over my life. I didn't think I could handle much more. I foolishly thought that things couldn't get much worst. I believed that I handled all that life could throw at me and live to tell the story.

William added drugs into his recreational life, on top of the drinking, that was already out of control. I never even imagined my life could turn out to be this way.

The drugs and the drinking proved to be too much for me and I was getting ready to end things for good this time. But before I was able to build up the courage to kick him out and end things, I learned that I was pregnant with our second child.

I didn't know what to do with my life at this point. How do I go on living with this irresponsible man who was still abusive and a lousy father to boot? Our son was nearly five-years old and, although I tried to shield him from it, he was starting to notice that things between Mom and Dad weren't so good.

Then God sent Wanda into my life. She was heaven sent and I was so grateful to have someone in my life that seemed to care about me. She lived in the apartment next door. The walls were very thin and she would hear at times what William would say and do to me.

I can't just blame everything on William. I was unhappy and frustrated and there were a lot of mistakes that I made and that only made things between William and I worse. Before I became pregnant with my second child Sometimes when Will would go out with his friends I would get a sitter and go out for a drink and party too. I just didn't know how to be better than I was at that time.

Wanda would come over and visit . She was a good friend that would care for me and offered me a shoulder to cry on . She was a working mother of two who always took time to check in on me.

Will and I were so immature and selfish. How could we possibly bring another child into our lives? Stuck in my sad reality, I began to focus on this new child that was on the way. The pregnancy gave me something positive to focus on.

I did want to have a little girl some day . Perhaps our son didn't bring us together the way a little girl could maybe, I thought. I enjoyed the relationship with my own father and dreamt that if I could give Will his own princess to love, maybe things would change.

William's reaction to the news of another child was surprisingly great. I knew that he wasn't what I would call "happy" in our marriage, but as far as I could tell he wasn't looking for a way out of it. Although he knew I wasn't happy, he was getting what he wanted out of our relationship. A baby would serve to further lock us into a co-dependency that happened to work for him, for the most part.

The other members of our family were equally delighted to have heard the news. If they had concerns about our relationship, they weren't telling us about them. Back in those days, every house was expected to deal with their own situations on their own.

Abusers are like ticking time bombs. It is not a matter of if they will hurt you again, it is a matter of when they will hurt you again.

When William was sober, he was a good man. There is good in all of us. I even felt like there were some similarities between William and Dad in that they both enjoyed drinking. The major difference was that my father never laid a hand on me to hurt me. William would push me around and hurt me from time to time, but I had learned to deal with those moments. The other difference was that my dad was a happy drunk. William's drinking emotions were like playing Russian roulette with a gun with one live round in it. You never knew when he was going to go off. Looking back, it began to feel almost normal.

But whenever Will mixed his drinking with drugs, the man simply was not in his right mind!

When I was seven months pregnant, William got upset about something. I can't even remember what the argument was about anymore. But he got so angry that he grabbed me by my hair and yelled at me. His face was beet red, as he yelled at me. I could smell the beer on his breath, but by the look in his eyes, it was more than just beer. He then dragged me by my hair across the living room floor. I kicked and screamed as he tossed me into my bedroom, as if I was a sack of potatoes.

I would call the police on him but he would usually be gone before they showed up. When the police would arrive, they would ask me if I wanted to press charges, but I couldn't do that to the father of my son, and soon-to-be child.

He would come back home a day later and he was always so convincing about how sorry he was. He would tell me that he loved me and how excited he was to see our new baby. And I believed him every time. I thought that was what you were supposed to do when your married; forgive each other and move on.

The calm after the storm was usually when things were best between us. Will was usually so grateful that I didn't have him thrown in jail that he would always be better to me and our son for a few days after an incident like that.

The day was finally here when my second child would enter into our lives. The labor for this child was easy in comparison to the first experience. My hopes were so high that my baby would be a girl this time.

My hope turned into reality when the doctor said the words I most wanted to hear, "It's a girl!" And she looked so perfectly beautiful .

My heart was overjoyed and filled with a special kind of love. It wasn't more or less than my first child but it was definitely different.

I laid in bed waiting for my husband to come and meet his daughter.

At that time, we had taken in a border in our home. A very gentle and friendly guy who'd found himself in the awkward position of having to call me that morning to tell me that he had to go to work—but there was a situation. William had not come home that night and if he left the house for work, my son Wilson would be left home alone. I remember feeling such sadness for my boy, my heart was crushed. I then called the man that was always there for us.

Dad came to the rescue, again, and picked up Wilson and spent the day with him.

I waited for an entire day. When Will finally arrived, he came in smiling and cheerful. He seemed to want to do better this time around.

But things wouldn't change. They would get predictably better after a big fight but then predictably worse when he felt like he wasn't in the dog house anymore.

A few months later, William and I thought it was time for us to go out on a date without the kids. We hired a sitter and we went to a house party with some friends. The night started out great and we were all having loads of fun, but it was getting late and I had to go relieve the babysitter. William had too much to drink, as usual, but he was one of those guys who never thought he was ever too drunk to do anything. Including driving!

As he stumbled to the car, I took the keys away from him and I told him that I would drive. I hadn't had anything to drink that night. He didn't like that arrangement and he insisted that he would drive us home. But as he tried arguing with me, I simply sat in the driver's seat, turned on the car, and yelled out, "Are you coming or are you walking?"

He was defiant as soon as we pulled off. He used colorful language to remind me that he was the man and that he was okay to drive. This was another one of those terrible incidents that he'd mixed the alcohol and the drugs.

He forcefully told me to pull over, but I wouldn't. All I wanted was to get us safely home. It was the dead of winter and it was snowing. We drove up to a traffic light and it was red, so I did what you are supposed to do at a red light, I stopped. In a fit of rage, William reached over put the car into park. He started reaching for the keys and I was trying to fight his hands off of them. We were shouting at each other as the situation felt more and more chaotic with each passing second. I was dealing with a mad man. He began trying to pull me out of my seat so that he could jump over into the driver's seat. When I didn't comply, he held me down and furiously began to punch my back with all of his might.

He was hitting me as if he were in a fight with another man. He had no mercy and showed no restraint. He hit me so hard that I was having trouble catching my breath. Foul words were flying out of his mouth as the punches continued to rain down on my back.

He then reached across my hunched body and opened the driver side door. He began to try to push me out of the door, but my seatbelt was still strapped. We wrestled one more time as I tried to keep him from unbuckling the seatbelt, but I was weakened by the beating he had given me. He threw me out of the car and into the snowy road that had not yet been plowed.

I laid there for a few minutes, hoping someone would drive by and help me. I couldn't believe what had just happened. I was in so much pain and badly bruised, too. I was able to pick myself up and walk to Wanda's apartment next to mine. I was too afraid to go into my own place because I didn't know where William was or if he would come home at all. I also didn't want my babysitter or my children to see me in that condition.

Wanda, my angel sent from God, took me in and helped nurse me back to health. She showed me such kindness and took such good care of me that night.

The next morning I could not even walk. It was a few weeks before I got my mobility back. I had suffered severe damage to my back that resulted in spasm that I have even until today.

Chapter 8

THE HURT
YOU CAN'T SEE

Recovery was slow and painful. But as bad as my physical pain was, it did not compare to how betrayed and heartbroken I was with William. I had seen him lose it before but he had never attacked me like this. How could he do this to me?

Every time I would close my eyes to rest, I would get vivid flashbacks of that few moments. On the rare occasions I could get comfortable enough to find sleep, I would wake up in a panic, breathing heavily, and afraid for my life.

Trying to care for two children all by myself for those few weeks with so much pain was very difficult, even with Wanda's help. William would try to come around and ask for forgiveness over and over again. It was as if he knew that he could wear me down.

This time he promised to help me with the kids and nurse me back to health. He actually told me that he wanted to take away the pain he caused me. It sounded sincere. William had his own brand of charm that always worked on me. Plus, I knew I couldn't make it on my own in my weakened condition.

My husband had been back for an entire month and life was grand. I began to feel better and we felt like a family, maybe for the first time. He was attentive to me and the children. We went for walks to the park and had picnics together. I was living the life I always imagined we could have together.

Late one night I was awakened by the phone. William wasn't home. Calls at that late hour rarely usher in good news.

It was William. He was calling from jail. He told me he was in trouble and his tone helped make it clear to me that this was not something he was going to get out of. He was arrested on drug and theft charges.

When I hung up the phone, I was struck with an idea that I didn't really even want to entertain at first. What if this was my chance to break free from him once and for all?

The next day I appeared in court to see him. I am not sure if I was there to support him or to see with my own eyes that he was getting locked up. He looked disheveled and tired.

The judge was a very serious man. As William stood before him, the judge was very brief and got right to the point. I was in a bit of a daze as the district attorney asked the judge to sentence him for six weeks. The judge agreed and they whisked him away.

William looked back at me as they took him away. I was wiping tears from my face as our eyes met. He probably thought those tears were because I felt bad for him. I did. But watching him get taken away to a place where he wouldn't be able to hurt me anymore brought a quiet relief to me.

As they walked him into the holding area and out of my sight, I began to notice that I was breathing. I know that is a weird thing to have noticed at that moment but it was probably the first time in years that I felt like I could catch a full breath. I closed my eyes and did it again. In then out. I was free!

Soon after, I sought the help of a Legal Aid/ Attorney. I didn't have much money but I was determined to file for legal separation. I remember her soft hands as she greeted me at her desk. She was a heavy-set, middle-aged woman with beautiful, long brown hair. She wore a very serious face but sometimes sported a kind smile. She had a very special smile. It made me feel comfortable instantly.

I told her my story and within minutes she began telling me not to worry. She assured me that I was safe now and that William wasn't going to be able to hurt me anymore.

She informed me that she was going to request that a bond (restraining order) be placed on William but then told me that I would have to appear in court in the presence of my soon-to-be ex-husband.

They brought him into the court room a few days later with handcuffs. I was sitting with my lawyer. She gave me strength. She didn't like what he did to me. She didn't care for William, not one bit.

I couldn't get myself to look at him for several minutes although I felt his fiery gaze on me. I finally got the nerve to look up. I glanced at him and he was wearing a ridiculous look of disbelief on his face. He gestured with his shoulders and hands as if to ask me why I was doing this. I was actually hurt by how shocked he was. Did he believe that I was so weak as to never stand up for myself or my children?

My lawyer told my story to the judge in a way that helped me realize how much I had endured at the hands of this person who claimed to love me. The judge granted the bond and the children were placed in my sole custody.

The judge made it clear to William that he was to stay away from me, even after he was released from prison. William acknowledged the warning and was taken away again.

My lawyer and I exited the courthouse and she gave me some final comforting words. The sun had been hiding behind some heavy clouds that day until the moment I started walking to my car. It's so hard to describe how good I felt as I walked away from the courthouse with the sun beaming on my face. It was as if God was smiling down on me. Just then I felt my smile fade slip away as I thought to myself, *He'll never let me go.*

The next few weeks were happy. I had the freedom I had always wanted. Wanda was around to help me. Dad stopped in to check in on me from time to time. Even William's mother called to check in on me. We shared a special bond.

My children didn't ask for their father. I suppose they had gotten used to him leaving for days at a time.

I am a little embarrassed to admit that from time to time I would catch myself thinking about William. He was the only man I had ever loved. It was hard not to think about him. I wondered if jail would change him. Maybe he would come out a different man.

When he got out of jail, he tried to come home but I told him that he was not allowed. He told me that if I let him in, than it wouldn't matter what the courts said.

After weeks of physical therapy and treatment, my back was finally getting better.

William continued to reach out to me and totally ignored the court order to stay away from me. I was determined that this time there would be no apology that would make me take him back.

Although he'd treated me so poorly and abused me so severely, William had what seemed to be a sick obsession with me. He just wouldn't, or couldn't let me go. There was a sinister element to his obsession. I didn't know it then but now I can see that it was demonic.

I knew that I wouldn't be getting my happy-ever-after storybook ending with William, but it felt as if Satan wasn't satisfied with just destroying our marriage, he wanted our total destruction.

One day I got a call from his mother. I was happy to hear her voice, but I instantly knew that something was wrong. She told me, "Your husband is in the hospital. He tried to commit suicide!"

She went on to tell me that if it weren't for a man working on a street light that noticed he was passed out in his car, William would have overdosed and died from the handful of pills he had taken.

My hands began to tremble. I was speechless. I couldn't say a single word. Then, my mother-in-law said, "Are you coming to see your husband?" She said it with compassion, not anger or judgement.

Her words were like a dagger in my heart. I loved his mom and the thought of her losing her son was unbearable. And I couldn't help but think that it was my fault that William had done this to himself. I was consumed with guilt. I was so cold with him. Maybe I didn't have to be so stern with him.

When I arrived at the hospital, William's family was huddled in the waiting room. My heart dropped as I thought it meant he had died.

Will's mom came to me and placed her hand on my face and with warmth she told me that he was waiting for me.

I walked into his room and there he was, the villain of my story, my abuser! But he was a broken man now. He opened his eyes and looked at me. He began to cry. He told me that he just couldn't live in a world where we couldn't be together. He reached for my hand. I hesitated. Then he truly began to weep like I had never seen him cry before. He was so heartbroken. He told me he was sorry. He swore he would change. He begged me to give him a reason to want to live.

And just like that, my heart of stone began to melt. He loved me! I felt an overwhelming sense of compassion towards him. I thought that I must still love him if I can still feel like this toward him.

I reached out to his extended hand. He gently pulled me towards him and we embraced. And without saying a word or ever dealing with our problems, we were "us" again.

The months that followed were special times in my life. He was helping with the kids. He loved to cook and prepared elaborate meals for our family and for our friends. He would cook for everyone. He was actually treating me nice.

I honestly thought it would last. If attempting suicide because you can't be with someone doesn't change you, nothing will.

After months of not drinking anything, he started drinking at home at first. He would stay home and watch movies with the kids and with me.

One of his friends started coming over, and they began having beers and watching movies.

His tone slowly started changing again. I got that sinking feeling that the good times wouldn't last. I felt him slipping away. His dark side began reclaiming the good man that had emerged. I warned him about it and he dismissed it. He told me I was over-reacting.

Within a year, William was back to staying out for days at a time. I was so disillusioned. I didn't even get angry when he would stay out any more. It was nice when he was gone.

Over the next year or so, he ended up in jail a couple more times. His drinking and drug addictions made him resort to stealing things. Each time he would go to jail I would try to break free from him.

It had gotten to the point that my love had turned into disdain for him. Whenever I would kick him out of the house, he would stalk me. He began following me everywhere I went. At night, I would look out the window and he would be sitting on a bench across the street drinking and watching my apartment.

I knew something drastic was going to happen. It had to, so that I could finally be free from him.

Chapter 9

MOM, I CALLED THE POLICE

*T*he scars from mental cruelty can be as deep and long-lasting as wounds from punches or slaps but are often not as obvious. In fact, an abusive partner doesn't have a problem with his or her anger but they have a problem with your anger. One of the basic human rights that William took away from me was the right to be angry.

He continued to stalk me and follow me. Whenever I had the nerve to say anything, he would ask me why I was so angry. My anger seemed to trigger his anger. He acted like I was the one with the problem. Everything was my fault, in his mind.

One day I was in my car with Wanda. She was driving. We pulled up to a traffic light, it was red.

William had been following us and we didn't even realize it. At the traffic light, he ran from his car to our car and began to scold Wanda for driving "our" car. He told her she had no right to drive "our" car.

One day while the children were in school, I was cooking and cleaning the house and I felt the presence of someone in the house. It was William. He somehow had picked the lock and walked right in. The moment I saw him, I ran for my life. He was there to harm me!

I ran down the back exit. I could feel his footsteps right behind me. He reached for me and grabbed my sweater. I wiggled out of it and kept running. I bolted out the back door and down the street. I ran as fast as I could. I felt like I couldn't outrun him. He was gaining on me. I ran until my lungs started burning and then I ran some more. I ran until I could not take another step.

When I finally stopped, I expected him to pounce on me but to my great surprise, he was gone. I didn't know when he stopped chasing me. I just remember feeling such relief.

Unhealthy love often degenerates into obsession. He wouldn't call it that. He insisted that he loved me. But how could loving someone bring so much pain and fear? If this is what love was, then I didn't want any part in it anymore.

I began feeling scared all the time. I was constantly looking over my shoulder. I felt like he was always watching me, even when he wasn't. My peace and my joy were gone.

I called the police so often that they recognized me by my voice. They always told me the same thing, "We can't do anything unless he is there right now, doing something to harm you."

At night, I would lock the doors then reinforce the doors with chairs. Sometimes, the last image I would see before going to sleep was William sitting outside on the bench across the street from my house.

One night after I struggled to fall asleep, I was awakened by a huge boom. By the time I had a chance to react, William was on my bed and he had a knife to my throat. He told me that if he couldn't have me, no one else would.

He covered my mouth with one hand and pressed the cold blade against my neck. My eyes were bulging out of my head. I thought that it was the end. The tears streamed down my face.

He told me over and over, "This is it! I am going to kill you!"

I managed to move my face so that I could speak. I told him that he didn't have to do it. I told him to think about our kids. I begged him to calm down.

But he had that wild look in his eyes. It wasn't even him. It was the presence of something much darker and more sinister. There was no humanity in his eyes, just an emptiness and a darkness.

My children were heavy sleepers. They had grown accustomed to listening to us fight. My greatest fear was that after he killed me, what would he do to the children?

I spoke to him in a very calm voice. Although I was more scared than I had ever been, I kept my cool. I tried to negotiate with him. I told him that if he put the knife down that we could talk. Maybe, in time, we might even get back together.

As I was trying to talk him down, I saw a shadow coming down the hall. It was my eight-year-old son. He slowly walked into view and our eyes locked. His father never looked back. William didn't see him.

I tried to communicate with my son with my eyes. All I wanted him to do was to call for help but I couldn't say a word to him. I tried to say it with my eyes. He and I always shared a strong connection and, in my desperation, I tried to send him non-verbal signals: "Call the police! Dial 911! Mommy needs your help."

William was capable of doing anything to anyone at that moment. My son seemed so brave to me at that moment. He didn't cry or even react. Without much expression in his face, he nodded at me and slowly walked away.

I was so relieved. I thought he had gone back to bed. At least he wouldn't watch his father murder his mother.

William had worked himself into a frenzy. He was swearing to kill me as he kept the knife at my throat.

"Why did you make me do this?" he cried. "I didn't want to have to kill you!"

I closed my eyes and my life flashed before me. I remembered my family. My siblings, my dad and even my mother. I felt so sad that I wouldn't get to see my children grow up and have families of their own. I also caught myself praying to God, as one does when their life is on the line.

I didn't really know how to pray, I just said, "Please, God, Help Me!"

A few moments later there was a ruckus at the door. It was the police.

It turned out that my son had not gone back to bed. He got the message! He went to the kitchen and called the police. He told him that daddy has a knife trying to hurt mommy and that someone should come and help.

William began to panic and pulled his hand away from my neck. I saw my opening. I shoved him off of me and I ran directly into the safety of the police. William was behind me trying to catch me, that's when the police grab him and push him up against the stove and searched him for the knife, because when my son called the police that night, my son told them "my dad has a knife and his going to hurt my mom". I guess that's why they came to my house so fast that night.

As they cuffed him and questioned him, he tried to make me out to be a liar. He told the police that he had no knife and the police could not find the knife I was describing.

He, so innocently, told the police that I was exaggerating. He said we had an argument but that he was in no way, shape, or form going to harm me or our family.

Without any proof, I feared that he was going to get away with it. We needed to find that knife!

William was so manipulative that he made everyone wonder if he was telling the truth. Was this just another domestic disturbance? I frantically pleaded with the police officers to keep looking. At that moment, he was the one who seemed sane and calm and I was the one that appeared to be a lunatic.

Then I heard someone in the bedroom say, "I think I found something!"

To my relief, it was the knife; the very knife that I thought he was going to use to end my life.

My son came running to me. "Mommy, I did what you said, I called the police!" Somehow he'd understood and even heard my voice telling him to call for help. I know now that it was God using my little boy to save my life.

They took him away. He was sentenced to four months in jail.

It wasn't much time but it was more than enough time for me to relocate my children and try to get a fresh start.

I would never take him back after that night. Whatever power he had over me was broken that night. Any speck of love that may have been lingering in my heart for William was gone. It was over! I was finally free!!!

Chapter 10

MOVING ON

William was sentenced to four months in prison. Four months may not sound like enough time, considering all the damage he was able inflict on me and all of the damage he wanted to do, but four months was enough time for me.

I was determined to sever all ties with Will. So we moved, again. My plan was to divorce Will and move on with my life.

With Will out of the picture for a while, life could find a new rhythm. My fears and anxiety slowly began to give way to happiness and peace. I was settling into a new life, free from the horror and drama that I had grown so accustomed to.

At least, that is what I was trying to convince myself of. There was a persistent fear, deep in my heart that William would find me once he was released from prison and never leave me alone. I felt like I needed security more than just putting a chair behind a locked door and certainly more than what the police could provide. Nothing seemed to deter him.

Try as I might, I couldn't hold on to my peace. With every passing day, I was getting closer to the day he would be released from prison.

Enter Ron!

My sister Agnes and I had always enjoyed a close relationship. Over the years, we would bring our children together. Her children Carrie and Jason and mine, They acted more like brothers and sisters than cousins. We were always together . I loved and cared for them like my own . We sometimes gathered friends and extended family at those family get-togethers.

Ron was a regular fixture at these hangouts because he was Agnes's brother-In-Law (Agnes's husband's brother). I had never really considered being with another man, but I was beginning to feel very lonely. William and I hadn't been together for a very long time. And now that he was gone, that feeling of loneliness intensified.

Ron was a good-looking man with a great laugh and an impressive physique. I may have caught him looking my way over the years but I had never allowed myself the indulgence of returning a look.

Ron was working on a Coast Guard ship and he was in pretty good shape. Perfect for a woman with an abusive ex-husband, I thought.

I'll admit it, I wasn't ready for a relationship. But at the time, I couldn't find the fault in my logic. If I had a strong guy next to me, William wouldn't mess with me anymore. I would have someone who loves me and I would have someone to love. I had never really been alone.

So, at the next family get together at Agnes's house, I made sure that Ron and I were alone for a few minutes and I let him know that I might be interested in him. He responded quite favorably so I did something a little outside of my comfort zone and asked him to come to my house for dinner one night. He agreed and we flirted the rest of the evening. It was fun, new, and exciting.

From the moment he arrived, there was electricity in the air. He and I shared a spark. I knew that the way to a man like Ron's heart was through his stomach, so I cooked him a juicy steak with all of the fixings.

No one had tapped into that side of me for quite some time. It felt so nice to be looked at the way he looked at me. He was a very good looking man.

We got to know each other better. He asked me about William. He knew him, obviously, but not well. I gave him the G-rated version of our story.

I asked him about his previous marriage. He told me that his wife could not adjust to him being away for months at a time, due to work, so she divorced him.

We talked about my children and he said everything I wanted to hear. He didn't have any children of his own but wanted someday to be a father. I thought that having Ron around my little family would be a good thing for all of us.

We started dating and it was a very happy time in my life. There was lots of compliments and nights out to dinner. It was only about a month before he told me that he loved me and I said it back.

He had a good job and started to take care of me the way I imagined a man was supposed to take care of the woman he loved. I was so eager to move on with Ron in my life that if there were any warning signs that Ron could be mean or abusive, I missed every single one.

When you have a couple of kids, you are surprised that any good guy would give you the time of day. Especially with William's voice still in my head telling me that no other man would ever want me, that I was used up, and that only he would ever love me.

After dating a couple of months, Ron started staying over.

There was a short adjustment period for us both but we were drunk-in-love so nothing phased us.

The day finally came when William was released from prison. Although I did not agree to see him personally, I thought it was only right to allow his children to see their father.

Their experience was horrible. They came home complaining about their dad smoking something that smelled very weird like skunk. They were devastated because, after four months of being away, he ignored them and made them feel like a bother to him.

So there I was again, hurt by William! But this time he did it by hurting the children. I was fed up. I knew what I had to do, so I did it.

My divorce was final while he was in jail, So The next day I was in court again and they awarded me full custody of the children.

Divorce is a loaded word. For some it represents the cataclysmic failure of a love. Divorce is accompanied by a host of negative feelings.

For others, divorce feels like someone that was a central figure in their story has died.

For me, divorce felt like total freedom. I wasn't sad or feel like a failure of love. I knew I had done everything I could do, and a whole lot I didn't have to do, to try to make my marriage work.

No one gets married to get divorced. But the years with William had been hard. The bad far outweighed the good. And as fate would have it, I got to keep the best things that came out of our union, my children. They were my world from the moment they came into it.

William wasn't so brave when he heard that I was with Ron. For the first time ever he respected boundaries. He was non-threatening. He was non-confrontational. My master-plan was working. I had found a good man that loved me and who helped keep the big bad wolf way.

A few months later, I noticed that my menstrual cycle was off. It was late which was very strange because I was taking birth control pills. I went to the doctor and it was confirmed that I was pregnant. Ron couldn't have been happier. He had started to believe that he would never have children of his own. This was the happiest I had ever seen him.

Ron decided that it was fate that brought this child into this world. If not a miracle, then a strange anomaly. How else could you explain getting pregnant while on birth control?

I thought Ron was doing just fine being the father figure to my two children, but this clearly meant something more to him than I even imagined.

His excitement brought a sense of newness to this pregnancy to me, too. I got to see everything through the eyes as a first-time parent. Everything was new to him. He wanted to be involved in everything that had to do with the baby. It was endearing.

Everything about this pregnancy was relatively easy. And with Ron's enthusiasm, nine months whisked by.

Our greatest concern was that Ron would be away at sea when our child would arrive. He would talk to my belly and tell the baby how much he loved him or her and how badly he wanted to meet him or her.

It was devastating to us both when he was called to work around the time of the baby's due date. This was the last thing we wanted. But it just so happened that while he was away, I went into labor.

As different and special as the pregnancy was, the labor felt quite familiar. I was delivering my third child without the father being present. But this time, it wasn't because of some weekend bender. Ron was a good man and wanted to be there more than anything. Our concerns about the job were legitimate.

Nature has her own clock and doesn't ask for permission or a copy of our schedules. It was delivery time and there was nothing stopping this child from coming.

This time, my dear sister Agnes and faithful friend Wanda were in the delivery room with me. I wasn't alone. They were such a great help to me.

A beautiful baby girl… Nicole!

Life is never a mistake. God doesn't create dupli-
cates, nor does He send life to the earth without fit-
ting that life with a unique destiny and plan.

Nicole, like my other two children, were sent
from heaven to me!

We were all resting comfortably at home when
Ron got back from his work assignment.

The first time he held Nicole, my heart wanted to
melt. It was as if Ron had found a new purpose for
living and her name was Nicole. He was amazed
by her and I have vivid memories of how he played
with her little hands.

I had a chance at living a normal life. Not that
there is anything normal about having three children. But we were happy.

When Nicole was nine-months old, Ron and I
decided to get married. We did everything at our
house. It had all of the thrills of an at-home wedding. We had family all around us, food and drinks
at the hall for the reception, and perhaps the most
important thing, My dad.

I remember being all dressed up in my pretty,
pink wedding dress with the cutest little veil and I
was waiting in my room for Dad to come to escort
me down. When the door opened and Dad saw me,

he looked at me with the pride that only a father carries for his little girl.

I remember thinking that it was my second wedding and that maybe I didn't deserve all of this beauty. I remembered how impersonal the City Hall's wedding festivities were with William. But that kind of negative thinking went away when Dad looked at me. He made me feel worthy. He validated my excitement by being excited himself.

He took me by the hand and asked me if I was ready. I took a deep breath and smiled.

We walked down the stairs as the music played and Dad brought me right to Ron, who was wearing a black suit with a black tie. He looked so sharp. They were standing next to the judge who was performing the ceremony.

Wilson, April, and Nicole looked so adorable. My life was finally coming together.

The following three years were awesome. We were a family. Ron and I got along very well. Every couple has their ups and downs, but we rarely fought. We were able to talk through our disagreements, which usually revolved around how he seemed to favor Nicole over Wilson and April.

I was willing to overlook much of it during this season of my life because I felt like I finally had a chance at happiness. He wasn't mean to the children, it was just an issue of favoring one child over the others.

But who could blame him? He was smitten by Nicole. She was his world.

Chapter 11

MY HEALER AND SAVIOR

The only residue left of my life with William was the occasional muscle spasms and flare ups that were recurring. At their worst, they were debilitating.

Ron and I were married nearly three years when I had the worst muscle spasms of my life. I was bedridden for weeks and I needed help even to go to the bathroom. The pain was impervious to the medication they prescribed to me. Nothing seemed to help.

I couldn't get comfortable, I couldn't sleep or even rest. I was miserable. There were some days that the pain was so unbearable, all I could do was cry and scream into my pillow. It was relentless pain.

During that three-week stretch of time, Agnes was a regular at my house. She helped me maintain the home and she was so helpful with the children. Ron helped too, but with his sporadic schedule, it was nice to be able to depend on my sister.

One night, as I was waiting for Agnes to come over to visit, I got a phone call from Betty, an older woman I had met with William's side of the family. She was another semi-regular card player. I knew her to be a very nice woman. I also knew that she was a Christian, but she never forced any of us to listen to her talk about it.

Betty told me she was checking in on me because someone had told her that I wasn't feeling well. When she heard my voice, she knew that something was terribly wrong. She politely asked me if I would allow her to come to my house to pray for me. I thought that the request was a little strange, but I was in so much pain, I figured that a little prayer wouldn't hurt me.

Agnes showed up and minutes later Betty arrived at my house. She wasn't alone. Betty came in with Jan…her secret weapon. Jan was a prayer warrior who enjoyed visiting the sick and praying with them.

Jan was short. She had a peaceful look in her eyes that was evidence of her walk with Jesus.

After initial introductions and some polite small talk, Jan asked if she could pray for me. She asked Betty and Agnes to come around the bed and she began praying .

Jan had an authority when she spoke. She wasn't loud but she was powerful. She was tiny but mighty!

As Jan prayed for me, she laid hands on me and I felt a tingle all over my body. It was as if there was fire being injected into my blood and it traveled all over. When I opened my eyes, I noticed a cloud in the room. Everything seemed blurry.

I began to cry. I realize that something was happening that went well beyond removing the pain I was feeling. My crying was cleaning my soul! Something had gotten a hold of me and I couldn't explain it. How could a cry feel so good? It was liberating.

Before I knew it, all four of us were crying. I had never experienced anything like this in my life. I wanted more and more of it. It was euphoric. It was a feeling of bliss that I never got from drinking or any other experience in my life. I was being filled with the power of the Holy Spirit but we had not yet been introduced.

I was trembling, but I wasn't scared. I was crying, but I wasn't sad. What had Jan done to me?

What happened next was nothing short of a miracle. Jan took me by the hands and told me to walk. I had not been able to walk in nearly three weeks and she knew that. But who was I to argue with the woman with the Jesus eyes?

So I got up from the bed, fully expecting to feel that old, familiar pain. And I was a little stiff at first. Jan told me again to walk back and forth again.

So I did. I walked from one side of the room to another. Gingerly at first.

"Again!" Jan commanded, "I declare healing in your body!" She prayed.

Back and forth I went. This time, it was noticeably easier.

Then something that felt like a rushing river sprang up from within me and took away all of my pain. But not just that, it removed the sadness that was attached to my pain. All of the hurt and sorrow that had been torturing me for so long was being washed away.

I began to cry again . I could feel the presence of the Lord in my room and I was in awe of Him!

For the first time in my life, Jesus was real to me. He was no longer just another fairy tale. Jan prayed to him, and He answered her. He was real, and I could feel His presence in my life.

Suddenly all of the Bible stories I'd heard when I was a child started to flood to the forefront of my mind. All of the sermons that I thought I hadn't paid attention to started ringing in my ears.

It was as if I was finding an old friend who'd been with me all along. I began to realize that all of my childhood experiences with church, Catholic and the Salvation Army, were depositing pieces of a puzzle that was finally coming together right in my own bedroom.

Jan asked me if I wanted to accept Jesus as the Lord and Savior of my life.

I whispered, "Yes, I do accept Jesus as my Lord and Savior."

At that moment, I realized that there was never a time when I was alone. He had always been with me. His presence was with me when I was sexually assaulted. He was with me when I was abused by my husband. He was helping me keep it together the times I thought I wanted to just end it all.

God was always in my life. The difference was, now I was ready to receive him. He was always trying to make His presence known to me.

Did I know exactly what accepting Jesus was? No! I just wanted more and more of whatever it was I was feeling. I felt light. I felt free. Something had been lifted from me.

That night, Jan asked Agnes the same question and Agnes accepted the invitation to follow Jesus too. We did it together.

Before they left, Betty and Jan invited Agnes and myself to attend their church. How could I say no? There I was, free from pain and feeling more alive than I had ever felt.

Looking back, I honestly don't know how much more of that pain I could have taken. I was so beyond what I thought I could bear anymore. God knew just when to knock on the door of my heart.

Agnes and I attended Betty and Jan's church, Victory Christian Center in St. John's. We were able to persuade our husbands to join us. We all loved the music and the people were so friendly. I couldn't believe that there were so many people like Betty and Jan. They all seemed to have this amazing relationship with Jesus and it made me want the same thing.

Within a couple of months our husbands both accepted Jesus as their Savior, too.

Although my salvation story was quite incredible, my actual walk with God was slow to get started. I was a bit of a skeptic. I believed in Jesus but believing in people took a little longer for me.

I wasn't as consistent in attending church at first. Partly because things with Ron had started to unravel around that time. The tension between Ron and my two older kids was beginning to create a massive wedge between he and I.

With Agnes's help and the encouragement of some new friends in the church, I started attending more regularly. My children accepted Jesus as their Lord and Savior, too. Our family was the talk of the church.

Eventually, I was asked to serve in the nursery and I said *yes*. Then I was asked to become an usher and I said *yes*. I loved serving people.

The kids got really involved in children's ministry and youth ministry. We were all on fire for God for a while but the men's enthusiasm began to taper off. They got to the point where they would attend only for special services and holidays.

My walk with God got stronger. And His power was overwhelming. But I have learned that there are some things that we can carry from our past without even knowing it. I felt God calling me to complete surrender but I didn't really know how to release old wounds and bitterness from a lifetime of abuse. That made things complicated with Ron. He was also dealing with trauma from his own life. I knew we needed help but neither one of us knew how to go about getting the help we needed.

Chapter 12

WORSE BEFORE BETTER

*I*f life has taught me anything, it is that you can only get out of life what you put into it. For the most part, if you sow love, you reap love. If you sow kindness, you reap kindness.

Galatians 6:7b says, "You will always harvest what you plant."

All of my good intentions and my lofty desires failed to bring me to a place where I was ever free to love Ron. There was still so much dysfunction in my life that I had never really surrendered to Jesus.

With my new-found faith, I started "believing" that things would just get better. I put so much faith in Christ, believing that He would turn everything around that I may have neglected to put in the hard work that I needed to do.

Ron became verbally abusive towards Wilson and April. Perhaps he was unhappy and they were the easiest targets. I don't know. But it exacerbated our relationship. I would pray for things to get better, but things only got worse.

My spiritual life had truly come alive and I felt an amazing closeness to God. But there is a difference between putting situations in God's hands and laying your life at His feet. It was clear to me that I wanted change. I just didn't know if I could let go of all of my baggage.

I was guilty of asking God for help without really being open for a change of heart. I was falling out of love with Ron. He was still a good man, but there had been words said that could not be taken back, on both sides.

I wasn't mad at Ron, I really felt like we had drifted apart and neither of us were doing enough to come back together.

Ron started sleeping in another room. After a while, we were living like glorified roommates. We talked politely to each other most of the time. We fought sometimes but for the most part it was a slow death. The passion was gone. No more dates or kind words. Love can't survive in a vacuum. Nothing can.

One day I heard Ron yelling at Wilson, as usual, and just as I was walking into the room, Ron told my son, "You are going to be just like your old man, good for nothing!"

Ron slowly turned around and noticed that I was in the room. I could see it in his eyes, he instantly regretted saying it, but it was too late. He knew that I would never forgive him for saying something like that to my son.

If anyone knew what I had been through with William, it was Ron. For him to compare "our" son to William was more hurtful than one of Williams slaps to the face. Words leave deeper scars than slaps. And Ron was turning into William more than Wilson would ever.

I wasn't really sure of Ron's feelings for my son at that moment . I know he didn't love Wilson and April the way he loved Nicole, but I didn't think he disliked them. I can't describe the hurt in my heart to finally see Ron's true feelings about my son.

What do you do when being a mom to your children is in direct contrast to being a wife to your husband? You should never have to choose between your husband and your child. But for me, at that time, the choice was simple, I chose Wilson and April over Ron. I am pretty sure I could have handled it better. Maybe there was a way I could have continued to love Ron and been a wife to him and try to restore the family that only months ago I thought was a happy one.

But here was the problem in a nutshell—when I pictured my future with Ron, I saw a life that eventually would fade out Wilson and April. When they got old enough, Ron would want nothing to do with them. I couldn't allow myself to accept a future where I could not see Wilson or talk to April whenever I wanted to. I could not reconcile with a man who didn't love or accept my children. They were my world.

We needed counseling. We needed someone to help us communicate. Perhaps someone could have helped Ron express his feelings about Wilson and April in a way that I could understand him. And maybe someone could have helped me explain to Ron that a mother like me could never separate herself from her children when they needed me the most.

So the children and I continued going to church. They were loving it and so was I. Church felt like such an escape from the sadness of home. Ron rarely came along.

The wedge between Ron and myself got worse. We had not slept in the same bed for months. He started staying out later after work. Most nights we would all be in bed before he got home.

To make matters between Ron and I even worse, William was trying, yet again, to be a dad to Wilson and April.

William surprised us all by writing a letter to April. In it, it expressed his desire to be her daddy. He told her how sorry he was for hurting her and begged her to give him another chance to make things right between them. April read the letter over and over. She cried each time she read it. She wanted to believe him, but she was scared.

April and I talked and I told her only if she wanted to. I explained that there was a chance that he might let her down, but loving someone always involves risk. I remembered the rare moments when William was at his best and when he was at his best, he was a good father. I wanted that for April. I hoped he could live up to the promises in the letter. My April desired to know the love of her father.

William was living with a woman at the time when April decided that she would stay with them for a weekend. It was one of the longest weekends of my life. I caught myself daydreaming about their time together. I was hopeful that the best version of William would show up. I imagined them laughing together and maybe April resting her head on her father's shoulder as they watched TV together. I prayed that God would protect April from whatever could go wrong as well .

I'll never forget the look on April's face when she came home that Sunday. She looked very sad. She tried hiding it at first, but a mother knows. I asked how her weekend was as she avoided eye contact with me and Wilson, who had come out of his room to see how April was doing. Wilson took one look at her and just went back into his room as he whispered, "I knew he couldn't change!"

I followed April into her room as she plopped into her bed—more angry than hurt at that moment. She was so upset with herself for believing him and falling for his lies one more time? William was drinking the whole weekend she was there .Once again she was very disappointed and hurt.

She was too young to know this depth of pain. It was so unfair. Ron was no help with April either. I guess he didn't know how.

I found myself struggling to defend my children from the men that were supposed to be there for them. The momma bear in me came out. My heart towards Ron grew even colder. I was Wilson and April's defender against the likes of William and Ron. I admit that I was not a good wife to Ron towards the end. I had issues of anger of my own too. And I resented him for his treatment of my children.

He retaliated by launching his own mental and verbal warfare against me. He was sharp with his words. He was no longer kind towards me. In fact, he could be quite cruel.

In my marriage to William I suffered physical abuse. In my marriage to Ron I suffered emotional and verbal abuse. Physical scars can heal after a while but emotional wounds can last forever. I could never fight back against William because he was much stronger than me physically. But I could match wits with anyone, including Ron. I gave as good as I got.

The marriage was over in my heart, but I was a Christian now. How could I just go out and get another divorce? I felt like I was supposed to keep up with appearances long enough for a miracle to happen. A miracle that I had stopped praying for.

I didn't want to be married to Ron anymore. There were some days that I would go for long drives and I would cry out to God to make a way of escape for me. As bad as our marriage got, I was ashamed that it would mean my second divorce.

Ron had told me that he had stopped drinking when we started going to church and I believed him. I knew that he might have an occasional drink here and there after work, but I believed it was well under control.

Until one night I had gotten up from a deep sleep to use the bathroom when, just then, Ron was walking in the door. He was drunk and his clothes were messy. He wasn't a messy guy.

I tried to pay him no attention but it all looked very suspicious to me. It meant very little to me that he had lied about the drinking. I couldn't get myself to care.

A few weeks later, I got a phone call from a friend who made some startling allegations about Ron's life outside of the house. The friend was convincing enough that it was all I needed to hear to finally come to term with reality. This marriage had been over for a long time and I was hanging on to nothing.

I wasn't hurt or sad. In fact, I was a bit relieved. I was ready for this chapter of my life to be over. It was only a matter of time.

I forgave Ron and we tried to stay together. The next few months contained some of my worst memories with Ron. We were mean and hurtful towards one another. He was even more vicious towards the kids.

Ron resented my going to church with the children and it became a point of contention. His resistance to church was his rejection of Christ and His love for us. But it was my continued connection to God and my church family that helped me make it through.

Ron was living the life of a single man. He would come and go whenever he pleased and didn't talk to me about anything he was doing.

I would do my own thing too. I had found a small network of families in my church who had children around the same age as my kids, so we would spend a lot of time together at each other's houses. It helped me deal with the impending end to this miserable marriage I was in.

My life was in a merry-go-round, but once I gave my heart to the Lord, I was never willing to turn away from Him.

I don't give up easily, but looking back, I was holding on to something that had died years prior. Ron eventually moved out and we got divorced. Ugh, another ugly divorce. But better an ugly divorce than a hateful marriage.

I was alone again. I would use this time to get closer to God. To live for him and to make him known to everyone I could.

Chapter 13

THE LONG WAY HOME

*T*he worst thing about divorce is what it does to the family—specifically, the children. Through no fault of their own, parents decide that separation and divorce is what is best for the two of them. And while some couples choose to stay together for the good of the children, it doesn't always work out for their good.

When Ron and I split, he didn't just divorce me, he also separated from his daughter and that hurt Nicole and me more than anything else. It was heartbreaking for Nicole.

I had to raise my children alone. I am not complaining about it. Being their mom is the greatest joy of my life. I deeply love them. It is amazing to me how uniquely I can love each one of them.

Nicole was 7, April was 12, and Wilson was 17.

For nearly all of their lives, I feared that my love, alone, would not be enough for them. How could I play the role of mother and father? It is my opinion that a mother can only be a mother. Meaning, as much as I tried, I could never be the father they needed. So I decided that I wouldn't try to be both. I would simply try to be the best mother I could be to them. With the help of God and my extended family, Pastor Harold Andrews and his wife (my friend Sybil) also their amazing parents showed us so much love.

When I gave my heart to Jesus, I was so blessed to know that God would step in to be their Heavenly Father. I wish that had been enough for me but as I look back now, I think I was always trying to find a companion who would love me enough to be a father for my children.

There was always a constant hint of selfishness in me that I always wanted and sometimes felt like I needed a man in my life. I already admitted that I did not enjoy being alone.

The next three years went by quickly.

I was very committed to two things, my family and my church.

I grew closer with the people at the church, I was committed to a prayer group with four ladies Ruth, Regina, Gloria and my sister Agnes That is where I got most of my healing and where God used me in prayer. These ladies were my trusted friends. Another trusted friend (my buddy) that God brought in my life Victoria. God will move through people. I enjoyed serving on the worship team, I served as usher, I served in children's ministry. I think I would have helped with shoveling the snow if they had asked. I loved hanging out with my church family!

I felt like I was able to detox from two extremely bad relationships. So when I thought I was ready, I began asking God to send me a Christian man. Someone who would share my values and my love for God and church. I knew I didn't want a man who didn't know the Lord.

I had been single for about three years, which felt a lot longer to me. Seemingly out of nowhere, I became friends with one of the men who in the church. He was exactly what I was praying for. He was deeply spiritual. I mean, this guy was a devout Christian. His love for God made me feel like I was a baby Christian. And I liked that about him.

I used to love having Bible studies with him. He was so knowledgeable in the Word. I thought that God had answered my prayer to the letter. Everyone at the church seemed to like him. So, once again, I moved forward into a relationship with blinders on.

We got close. Too close. Too fast. Before I knew it, I was being sucked into the vortex that was Joe.

It was only Nicole and I at the time, Wilson and April were already off on their own. Joe swooped in and began to smother me and eventually became extremely controlling. If William was physically abusive and Ron was verbally abusive, Joe was spiritually abusive.

He used his knowledge of the Word to subjugate me. He tried to lord his God-given leadership position as the head against my femininity. He used such flowery words that it was hard to argue with the way he phrased his biblical arguments. They were so convincing and I was outgunned. I felt myself falling into the trap of spiritual abuse. He started trying to control where I went, who I talked to, and what I did.

I thought long and hard about even including him in my story. Being with him was a clear mistake that I wish I could simply erase. It was a blip on the radar that is my life story. But when God asked me to write this book, He told me that he was going to use the good and the bad of my life to minister to people.

If my life story is a cautionary tale for women and men about abuse, pain, and God's redemptive plan, then I needed to include this part of my life.

I don't see a lot of statistics about men using what they consider spiritual authority to dominate and sometimes abuse their feminine counterparts. But there are plenty of statistics regarding male chauvinism and sexism.

I want to go on the record as saying that I happen to believe in the order that God established in scripture in 1 Corinthians 11, "The head of every man is Christ and that head of every woman is the man."

But what happens when the man who is trying to enforce his dominance over a woman is not submitted to Christ? That is a scary situation and one that I needed to get out of in a hurry. But I didn't know how to break free of this relationship.

If I disappointed him, he wouldn't speak to me for weeks. I wasn't aloud to make decision of my own . He was militant in his ways. I didn't want to just end another relationship. After all, this man was a "good Christian" as I thought. I wanted to be happy I'd found him.

Except I wasn't happy, at all.

My daughter and I went to the Dominican Republic for a wedding. I was in desperate need of a getaway and it would be a great time for us to simply enjoy each other. Nicole was being negatively impacted by Joe's ways.

The trip started like a dream vacation but ended as a nightmare, because midway through I got very Ill . I some how picked up some kind of bug infection in the water or food. 13 years ago prior to this time I was diagnosed with Ulcerative Colitis (UC). I won't bore you with the details but in a nutshell, Colitis is a disease that attacks your intestines and makes your life very difficult and painful. This infectious bug flared up the colitis and I became extremely Ill.

When we got back home, I couldn't really eat. The pain was unbearable. I had lost nearly thirty pounds in a matter of weeks. The doctors were concerned because they couldn't seem to get this thing under control. I was in and out of the hospital and there was no end in sight.

With all that I had been through, you might be surprised to hear that it was during that particular time period was when I struggled most against the spirit of suicide. There was such darkness trying to overtake me. The pain was unrelenting and there was no hope in sight.

There were some nights that I told the Lord to just take me with him. I wished I would fall asleep and drift off into eternity with Jesus.

Thank God for my Pastor . He was there for me and my children all the time. He is my spiritual father Even to this day. If it were not for them I don't know if I would even be here. The love and support they showed me was supernatural. The love of God that flowed through them was so genuine and authentic.

When medicine and treatments weren't working, their prayers and our church family helped give me the strength to keep fighting. When my depression told me that this would be the end, my pastor's love and prayers helped pull me out of the darkness.

It was because of them that I decided to take the long way home. Meaning, I rejected the darkness and ignored the sinister voices that were trying to cut my journey short. I learned how to choose life.

Nicole was also a great source of strength for me. When the deepest darkest thought of suicide invaded my mind, Who would raise her I thought. I didn't choose to die because I wanted to live for All three of my children.

The only good thing that came out of this sickness was the end of my relationship with Joe. It took having a near-death experience for me to finally decide that I was not going to settle for being *almost* happy anymore. I had finally come to the place that I would rather be alone, as much as I hated it, than to be stuck in a dead-end relationship.

After a few months of begin sick every day, I slowly started to recover. Food was still making me sick, but I believe that prayer made all the difference in the world. Until finally, I was healed.

Colitis is said to be a chronic, life-long disease, but by the grace of God and faithful prayers I am healed.

Throughout my life, God has always provided for me. He has given me favor in jobs by putting me in positions that I wasn't necessarily qualified for but somehow I was called for.

I worked with the Canadian Blood Service as a clinical assistant with no medical background. I wasn't a phlebotomist but I was drawing blood and running simple tests for patients all the time. I loved that job because I felt like I was able to have a personal impact on people. My faith and positivity impacted their lives. I prayed for every patient within myself and sometimes out loud if I felt like they really needed it.

I also worked as an Ambassador for West Jet Airlines in the customer service department. I directed people towards their gates and helped to check people in for their flights. This was another job that I truly enjoyed because I was able to make complicated travel easier for people. Plus I got fantastic travel perks that would come in nicely later in my story.

But one of my all-time favorite jobs I ever had was when I worked for VOAR Christian Radio Station as a DJ. Who would have guessed it, right? Me? A DJ?

It was a request show every weekday for two hours a day. I would talk and take requests and people would call in and I would pray for them. I was so humbled by the sheer number of people who would call in to the program to make musical requests or ask for prayer .Especially how the Lord would regularly fill my mouth with words of wisdom for every situation.

It was amazing to think about how many people I was able to reach with God's love each and every day. The testimonies would just pile in with people saying that I played the right song at just the right time in their lives. They would be so thankful that I shared a particular scripture because they heard God speak to them at the moment that they needed it most.

And being on the radio was the first time I was able to take some of my life experiences and use them to minister to other people. I was shocked and amazed how my life was helping other people.

God is indeed amazing! Only He could take all of my pain, emotional hurt, and abuse and use it for the good of others. And when God started using my past to bless others, I started finding healing in the sharing of my testimony.

There are times when I wish I had not gone through any of it, but when I see God use it to help someone else break free from an abusive relationship, I give God all of the Glory. I found that when I put my life in His hands, He doesn't just use the good parts for His glory. God redeems the pain of our lives by using it to help others.

Chapter 19

SAD GOODBYES

$\mathcal{M}$y father was a constant figure in my life. I could have told you countless stories and given hundreds of examples of the many ways he was there for me throughout my life. It doesn't matter how old a girl gets or how many children of her own she has, you never outgrow being Daddy's little girl.

But Dad was older now and the many years of heavy drinking had damaged his body, especially his liver.

Dad was small in stature but he was larger than life. Then, seemingly out of nowhere, he started losing weight and could not keep food down. I was with him when his doctor told him that he had to give up drinking because of the serious damage it had done to his liver. He seemed really somber at

143

the moment and I thought that he understood the severity of his condition.

Dad said all the right things and did all the right things…initially. But after a few months, at a family get together, I caught him sipping from a flask he was carrying. It became clear to me that this was a fight that he would not win.

Two year's went by; his condition deteriorated even more. He barely tried to eat because his stomach couldn't handle solid foods anymore.

On one of my Sunday visits with Dad, My daughter April and I sat and observed him sitting on his chair as he watched TV. He looked sick and frail. He was a shell of the man he once was. Part of the issue was that he was an old man now, but I knew that the drinking was robbing him of whatever good years he could still have with all of us.

My eyes welled up with tears as I was faced with the inevitable demise of my beloved dad. It is almost unthinkable. We usually reject the idea of losing our parents because it brings us face-to-face with our own mortality, it seems to me. I could have easily gone into denial about what was happening. I could have just prayed and asked God for another miracle.

Instead, I dried my tears and shook off all of the negativity and told my dad that we were going to the hospital. I wasn't going to let him go without putting up a fight!

He tried to refuse but he recognized the look in my eyes. He had seen it so many times before. He just couldn't refuse a request from me when he saw all of the love and admiration I had for him. It was my genuine concern for him that made him agree to go with me.

When we got to the hospital, Dad was admitted at once. Things moved quickly after that. After about a week in the hospital, Dad looked to be in really rough shape. Every treatment they tried didn't work and, with each passing day, dad got worse. Eventually, Dad had intravenous lines and was heavily medicated most of the time.

My sisters, my daughters, and I took turns caring for Dad for the more-than-three weeks he spent in the hospital.

One morning, as Dad's doctor was making his rounds, he came in to see him then asked me to step outside into the hall with him. I kissed Dad on the forehead and walked outside.

"I know you don't want to hear this, Linda," he said, "But your dad isn't going to get any better."

I looked at him and smiled. I heard what he said, but it didn't register. He asked me if I'd heard him. I nodded my head, yes, but he knew I was having trouble with what he had just told me.

He said, "Linda, call the family and prepare them for what's coming." I snapped out of the daze and initial shock and got right to it. There was no time for sorrow.

I called my sister Agnes and she came immediately. More calls to all of my siblings and they all started making arrangements to come see Dad.

I called Mom to tell her that Dad was dying and her reply was her typical oh, but I could tell Mom's heart stopped a beat. She was quiet, she simply acknowledged what I said and hung up the phone. She did come to visit him.

My son Wilson lived in Alberta and as soon as he heard the news, he made immediate plans to come say goodbye to his grandfather. Dad and Wilson shared a special bond. Dad helped me raise Wilson for the first couple of years and they just kept that special connection.

Finally, everyone made it to the hospital. My sisters and brothers were there. All of my children were there, with Wilson being the last to arrive. It felt like Dad was hanging on until Wilson showed up.

My daughter's and everyone loved listening to Dad's stories and we were looking for ways to cheer him up. So, we suggested that Dad tell the story of when he first met Mom. We had all heard it many times, but it had always made him happy to tell it.

He took a deep breath and talked about walking into the store and seeing the girl with the red coat and red lipstick. It was love at first sight!

He smiled and the entire room lit up. It was if the cloud of death lifted for that brief moment.

Mom and Dad had been divorced for a long time, but neither one of them ever remarried. They were connected somehow. We would have family events and they would be together. Dad would still try to flirt with Mom from time to time, but she never responded.

A couple days later, things took a turn for the worse. It was the end.

We were gathered all in the room again and the nurse gave Dad another high dose of morphine to make him comfortable. He was just laying there with no life in him. Hours went by and when the room was quiet, I went over to his bed side just to be close to him .He looked at me at that moment and it was as if he was asking me if he was dying through his eyes.

I told him "yes dad you're going to be with Jesus now." He blinked his eyes. as if he understood what I was saying. There wasn't a dry eye in the room. It was the saddest moment of our entire lives. Later that evening, he acknowledged that death had come for him and he had found peace.

When Dad took his last breath, we all held on to ours. Time stood still. No one moved or made a sound.

My life flashed in front of my eyes and I saw Dad in almost every important moment of my life. I remembered Dad as a young man holding my hand as we would go for our walks, the sound of his laughter filling a room, his voice crying on the phone asking me to come back home, talking to my baby Wilson, walking me down the aisle at my wedding, dancing with my children at family

Christmas party's... all of that and so much more, I saw in a millisecond. When I snapped out of it, he was gone.

All I could hear in the background was the sound of family members crying. I had tried to keep strong while he was ill, but at that moment, I just lost my strength. I wept! I felt my knees buckle. There are no words to describe the incredible sadness of losing a parent. Only others who have lost a parent can truly identify with this kind of heartbreak.

In all of the sadness of dad's passing, I realized that his last gift to the family was bringing us all back together as we leaned on each other like we had never done before.

Dad's funeral was at the Basilica, the biggest church in St. Johns. They brought him in, accompanied by The Royal Newfoundland Regiment ceremonial bagpipes. My brothers, my son, and nephew carried him into the church. There were so many people that I hadn't seen in years. The priest performed a lovely service, which included Nicole reading a scripture.

At the gravesite, they gave my brother Jimmy the Canadian Armed forces flag that was placed over our dads casket . It was a touching time for everybody.

I didn't really grieve after Dad passed because I was trying to be strong for everyone. But it weighed so heavily on me that I ended up speaking to a therapist. She listened to me talk about Dad and my life. It might sound silly to some, but she gave me permission to grieve.

For a while, I remained sad. After a few sessions, the doctor prescribed a medication that made me feel loopy and made everything seem foggy, so I didn't take them for long.

I decided to take my sadness to the Lord. The Holy Spirit taught me to thank God for Dad's life instead of feeling sorry that he was gone. After a while, I was able to think about Dad and, instead of breaking down and crying every single time, I started smiling and thinking about where he is now.

I still felt the sadness of his loss, but sadness was not all I felt, there was more than that. I felt so blessed that he was my father. He wasn't perfect, but over the course of my life, he was one of the only men who demonstrated true love to me. And for that I am so grateful.

Agnes and I were at my mom's bedside when she took her last breath twelve years later. Mom was in a home and, with Dad gone, my attention instinctively went towards developing my relationship with her.

A few years before she died, my heart softened towards her. I told her so often that I loved her, until I started hearing it back from her. I would visit as much as I could and bring Mom candy and chocolate when I visited her. The home she was in was a beautiful estate with plenty of room to walk around. She used a walker to go everywhere because she couldn't sit still for too long.

Whenever I would visit, I would ask one of the nurses and they would tell me where I could find her. We would sit outside and chat a bit. Some days, I would bring her a meal from the outside world and we would enjoy some food together. Sometimes I took her for day trips to the mall or for a drive so we could talk.

Mom never did change who she was, but I was able to make peace with her personality and character.

I was able to understand her upbringing more, which also helped me understand the decisions she'd made in her life. As we get older ourselves, we get a little wiser.

Deep down, I knew I had to forgive her for leaving Dad all those years ago. I suppose I resented her for choosing to stay away when my sister and I'd returned to Dad when we were still just little girls.

With the life experiences I had with William and with Ron, I was now perfectly able to understand when a woman refuses to subject herself to any further abuse. Dad never directly abused mom, but his drinking was too much for her to handle. Who was I to hold her to a higher standard than I held myself to? So, in my heart, I forgave her.

On Mom's last birthday, my sisters and I brought her a meal from her favorite restaurant. We went into the big room and it was Mary & Jack's girls together again.

My siblings and I had the blessed gift of ushering mom into the Lord's presence. She died peacefully and quietly. I imagined Dad being part of the welcome committee in heaven for mom. The very thought of it makes me smile.

Chapter 15

TO LOVE AGAIN

I was visiting my friend Roxanne one evening and our conversation went towards the topic of love and happiness. I confessed to her that although I didn't like being alone, I didn't want to get involved with another wrong guy!

My life experiences suggested to me that maybe I wasn't ever going to win in the game of love. I wondered out loud that perhaps there was something wrong with me.

Roxanne flatly rejected the notion. She knew me well enough to see the transformational work that God had done in my life. She reassured me that I was no longer the same person and that I shouldn't close the door on love.

We talked and prayed about it and then Roxanne brought up the idea of internet dating. I nearly spit out the coffee I had just swooshed into my mouth. Me? On an internet dating site ?

In my private prayer time, I was telling God that I just want to be loved and have someone to love and cherish till death do we part. I was specific in my request to God by asking for someone that fits me and my family.

Within a matter of minutes, Roxanne had her computer open and she was walking me through a Christian dating site. I acted disinterested but something was stirring inside of me. I was fighting back my nervous excitement.

Before I knew it, Roxanne had created a profile for me and we started looking at pictures of eligible bachelors. I quickly clicked past a few guys and we were making little jokes about what it felt like to online shop for a husband.

Then, Daniel's profile appeared. I told Roxanne to wait a minute. He was handsome and looked very kind. Something about his profile picture captured my imagination. But then I noticed that he lived five-thousand miles away.

I asked Roxanne what I should do if I was interested in him. She told me that I could send him a message or send him a wink. I figured that because he was so far away that a little wink would be a cute way to flirt, but I thought I wouldn't hear back from him.

He replied with a simple, "Hello!"

I then noticed that his profile stated that he was a worship leader. That intrigued me because I had recently joined the worship team and found it to be immensely rewarding.

Roxanne noticed right away that I was a little smitten and we joked a little more about it.

Daniel and I started talking on the phone. The conversations were fun and often spiritual. There is a certain freedom in getting to know someone that you may never have to see face to face. So we said things to each other that we might not have said under normal circumstances. We did have a lot in common. And there was honesty and a freedom in our conversations that I found really refreshing.

After the initial glow of getting to know each other wore off a bit, the conversations became fewer and more far between. Then, for no specific reason, we just stopped talking for a while. We were both living busy lives and I chocked it up to the distance and maybe a case of bad timing.

Several months had passed since we'd heard from one another, when Facebook suggested Daniel as a friend to me.

We reconnected and we talked more frequently than before. We had both been through so much in our past that although we knew we liked each other, we decided to take it slow.

We had been talking for nearly two years before we actually met in person. Interestingly enough, Daniel happened to live relatively close to my father's side of the family in California. That was the same family that used to visit us in St. Johns when I was a kid. We had remained close through the years.

At the time, I was working for West Jet and flights were heavily discounted for me, so I decided to visit my Sweet amazing Aunt Dot and my cousins Debbie, Ronny and Ray. who lived in Napa Valley, which was conveniently only two hours away from where Daniel lived. I also had my uncle Bob and aunt Sylvia and more cousins Sharon, Brian and David whom lived not far from Daniel in Morgan Hill. I would get to see them all!

My nerves seemed to get the best of me once I got to my aunt's Dot's house, because I had been there almost three days and I had not called Daniel yet to let him know I was so close.

A couple of days before I was returning back home, my Aunt Dot told me that If I leave without making the call and trying to meet Daniel face to face I would probably regret it. She emphasized that meeting him was something I wanted to do while I was there. I knew she was right.

I called him and Daniel insisted on taking me to dinner that very same night. We met and I was a little surprised at how comfortable it all felt. We talked for hours on end. He asked if he could see me again the following day and take me to the airport. I agreed and we spent another lovely day getting to know one another.

As I was boarding the airplane to head back home, I was thinking on how much I enjoyed our time together and I may not ever see him again. So I wanted to say a final goodbye.

I sent him a text saying *thank-you* for an amazing couple of days, it was so nice hanging out with you in Califorina.

He replied, "What are you doing for Christmas? I want to visit you in Newfoundland!"

He booked a bed and breakfast for the holidays and spent ten days meeting the family, sightseeing around St. John's, and meeting my church family.

He got the thumbs up from everyone he met. Well, almost everyone. My children loved and cared for me so much, they were not on board with this yet.

After only a few months, Daniel asked me to come visit him again, so I did. By this time we had been talking on the phone for nearly three years, but we had only seen each other twice. This was our third time together. I came to visit again .He prepared a beautiful dinner for me in his home and after dinner, he asked me to marry him.

I was taken a bit by surprise and I wondered if he was joking with me. I answered that he didn't even have a ring, which was my way of asking him if he was serious.

Daniel said to me, "I'll be right back," and he left for the other room. When he returned, he came back with a ring! My eyes shot wide open as I wondered how in the world he'd guessed my correct ring size. Is this really happening!

I looked into his eyes and tears began to flow from my own eyes and I said, "YES!"

I flew back home and made plans to move to California. Everything seemed to progress rapidly, but there was such a peace in my heart about how God seemed to orchestrate everything.

I mentioned our engagement to my family from Napa, They all were so happy for us. My cousin Brian and his wife Lynn, who lived in Morgan Hill, generously allowed me to live with them for four months in their sprawling home, until Daniel and I got married. And as if that was not enough, my family in Napa threw a lovely engagement shower for us.

Living there, at Lynn and Brian's house, for those four months was amazing. They would go off for the day and I was able to take in the incredible sights. I felt so protected and loved by God. They even lent me a car so that I could get around. They did all of that for me and never asked for anything in return. Being with them and the all of my Napa family made me miss Dad so much. They embodied what family was supposed to feel like.

A church member at Daniel's church offered to host our wedding in their amazing home. We didn't have to pay for very much . We only had to pay for food for the BBQ, but everything else was taken care of and served by Daniel's church family. Out of that church family I met such amazing life long friend's and one of them became my best Califorina buddy, Leslie and I became like sister's, there's nothing we wouldn't do for each other. Daniel's landlord even volunteered to be the grill master of the BBQ.

It was like nothing I had ever experienced.

My cousin Brian walked me down the aisle. Daniel was playing guitar and singing a song as I came down. All the guests lovingly watched as I walked to Daniel.

It was at that moment, as I was standing before Daniel, I finally knew what *forever* meant. It felt like none of it was real. It was like a dream.

I was afraid that something might happen to wake me from the most perfect dream ever. It had been my experience that nothing good would last forever. But it wasn't a dream. This was my life and it was all happening in real life. I was in awe over it all.

Today, Daniel and I live back in Canada. We have been happily married for nine years. My children, who initially were reluctant to accept a stranger, have come to love and accept Daniel in my life and in theirs.

The journey of my life has not been an easy one. We both made a few mistakes along the way, but we are so thankful for the grace of God.

As I look back on my life, I can now see the hand of God working throughout my entire life. God was loving me far before I even acknowledged His existence.

I would have never thought that I would find the love of my life at the age of fifty. Apparently, God has a pretty good sense of humor, too.

Chapter 16

THOSE WHO HOPE
IN THE LORD

I still have moments when I feel rejected or betrayed. Even when you manage to move beyond your past, you can never really shake all of the trauma. They are embedded in your memories and in your emotional history.

What I have found to be true is that God overturns prior rulings from our past that were against, into favorable rulings on your behalf. The pain that others caused us doesn't have to define us or limit us for the rest of our lives. When a person surrenders to Christ, God sits as a judge and there is a re-trial for each case of your past and He rules on your behalf.

Those bad things that seemed to have only hurt you, God is going to work them out for the good.

My favorite Bible verse is Isaiah 40:31, "But those who hope in the Lord will renew their strength. They will soar on wings like eagles; they will run and not grow weary, they will walk and not be faint."

what Isaiah 40:31 verse means to me. Over the years, I have learned to soar like an eagle, high above the problems and circumstances of life, and get close to the Son, who renews my mind, heals my body, and restores my soul.

As I think about my life I can say these few statements without hesitation…

- <u>I don't have any regrets</u>. Are there a few things that I wish I could change about my past? Sure! Who doesn't? But I have come to embrace the life I have lived, mistakes and all. They have made me into the woman I am today. And I *like* who I am, now.
- <u>I owe it all to God</u>! Accepting Jesus and my Savior was the single most important decision that I have ever made. He has redefined what life means to me. He has given my entire life a redeeming purpose. Without him, I would be another bitter and battered woman trying to find the meaning of it all.

The bible says in I John 1:9, "If we confess our sins, He is faithful and just and will forgive us our sins and purify us from all unrighteousness."

God can and will do for you what he did for me. I am a living miracle and I am proof positive that the love of God can heal your broken heart and restore your life by giving it meaning and purpose.

If you want to allow God's power to fill your life with love, pray this prayer with me: "Dear God, I am a sinner. I'm sorry for my sin; please forgive me. I believe Jesus Christ is Your Son and that He died for my sins and You raised Him to life. I want to invite You into my heart to take control of my life. In Jesus' Name I pray, Amen."

I do recommend that you find a good church family near you and watch God begin to change your life for the good.

My life is far from perfect, but I would not trade it for any other. I am so grateful and blessed for what the Lord has done for me.

Daniel and I have challenges just like every other marriage. But with God's help, we work them out. One of the things Daniel does whenever I feel a little hurt or feel a little fearful, is that he lovingly pulls me back and asks me how he can make things better for me. He is a good man who is always willing to fight for our love, even when I feel like running away.

I thank God every day for my three children. While I was raising them, I prayed that God would help them be great people, despite all that they had endured and seen. God has been so good to me in that each and every one of them is not just someone that I love as a child, I love them for the people they are. God was their father and he helped me raise them.

Wilson is a Correctional Officer in a Penitentiary and he is married to his soul mate, Jaclyn. They gave me two awesome grandchildren, Michael and Emily. Wilson is an amazing husband and father and turned out to be total opposite from his earthy Dad.

April married Mark, an awesome and loving man. She is an amazing hard working lady and has a very rewarding job with the government. I am so proud of her devotion to her family. She and Mark gave me a gift called Madison, my third grandchild.

Nicole is another amazing lady, she is my inspiration to write this book. She happens to work for the The Gideon International Canada & ShareWord Global, she also works for the Billy Graham ministry. She literally married a rock star. His name is Christian and his band is called Informants. Nicole and Christian travel all over the place spreading the love of God.

Each spouse fits them so perfectly. I am so satisfied with what God has done for our family.

When Daniel came into my world, he also brought me the gift of a beautiful and very intelligent young lady—Danielle, my bonus daughter. Danielle has an amazing career in San Francisco. Daniel's Sibling's and their families are also gifts to me and I love them all.

I am also so content that my brothers Robert, Jimmy, and Eddy, and my sisters Agnes and Lillian, they all have beautiful amazing families as well, whom I love so dearly.

This young teenage girl not knowing her self-worth is a different woman today. Stay strong and know that God is always there to rescue you through you're journey.

God continues to surprise me with how he uses Daniel and me every day. God is already laying the foundations of more exciting chapters of our lives

CPSIA information can be obtained
at www.ICGtesting.com
Printed in the USA
LVHW012100100520
655322LV00015B/2191

9 781545 656211